WINNING

THE WAR WITH

YOURSELF

FIELD MANUAL

Using Timeless Principles of Military Strategy
to Defeat Your Own Worst Enemy

JOE TYE

CEO and Head Coach, Values Coach Inc.

Winning the War with Yourself

Quantity discounts are available: call Values Coach at 319-624-3889

ISBN#: 1-887511-37-7
ISBN 13#: 978-1-887511-37-7

Cover design and interior layout: Studio 6 Sense • studio6sense.com

WAR IS HELL...
LIFE SHOULDN'T BE

WINNING THE WAR
WITH YOURSELF
FIELD MANUAL

"Know the enemy, know yourself; your victory will never be endangered. Know the weather, know the terrain; your victory will be total."

Sun Tzu: *The Art of War*

"I count him braver who overcomes his desires than him who overcomes his enemies; for the hardest victory is the victory over self."

Aristotle: Ethics

"I cannot consent to place in the control of others one who cannot control himself."

Robert E. Lee: *Letters of General Robert E. Lee*

"In combat the only thing more accurate than *enemy fire* is incoming *friendly fire*."

Murphy's Laws of Combat

"The Warrior Ethos recognizes that each of us…has enemies inside himself. Vices and weaknesses like envy and greed, laziness, selfishness, the capacity to lie and cheat and do harm to our brothers. The tenets of the Warrior Ethos, directed inward, inspire us to contend against and defeat these enemies within our own hearts."

Steven Pressfield: *The Warrior Ethos*

For Steve Pressfield

Who showed us the true nature of the enemy

ALSO
BY JOE TYE

Never Fear, Never Quit: A Story of Courage and Perseverance

Staying on Top When Your World's Upside Down

The Twelve Core Action Values

The Florence Prescription: From Accountability to Ownership

All Hands on Deck: 8 Essential Lessons for Building a Culture of Ownership

The Cultural Blueprinting Toolkit

Leadership Lessons from The Hobbit and The Lord of the Rings

The Healing Tree: A Poet, A Mermaid, and A Miracle

Your Dreams Are Too Small

ADVANCE PRAISE FOR

Winning the War with Yourself Field Manual

"This is a masterful piece of writing that is applicable to all people, regardless of their life circumstances. The daily battle we all face against 'YOWE' (Your Own Worst Enemy) can bring down even the strongest amongst us. But Joe offers enduring, timely and actionable tips to flip YOWE in your favor. Read this book now! If you are like me, it will become one of your go-to sources for navigating through the vicissitudes of life."

David Altman, Ph.D.
Executive Vice President and Managing Director
Europe, Middle East and Africa
Center for Creative Leadership

"Great coaching can help you face your most important life challenge – learning to manage yourself! Imagine having some of history's most successful commanders serving as your own personal coaches to help you accomplish that. This is a wonderful guidebook on how to do more by being more!"

Marshall Goldsmith is the Thinkers 50 World's #1 Leadership Thinker and is the #1 *New York Times* best-selling author of *Triggers* and *What Got You Here Won't Get You There* – two of Amazon's '100 Best Leadership & Success Books to Read in a Lifetime' list

"Deploy out any one of the strategies described in this book and you will be far more effective at achieving your goals. Deploy the right combination of strategies and you will become unstoppable."

Gary Ryan Blair, The Goals Guy, author of *Everything Counts* and creator of The 100 Day Challenge

"If you hope to become the person you imagine you could be, read this book."

Dan Rockwell, Leadership Freak, Coach, and Presenter

"You'd have to live a couple lifetimes to read all the books and distill the wisdom that Joe Tye has captured in this amazing text. He's done the heavy lifting. It's your turn now to sit and absorb lessons and insights that range from Roman generals to current military leaders. You'll discover YOWE (Your Own Worst Enemy) and how it can conquer you and – even better – you can prevail over it. Practical. Provocative. Personal. Pertinent. Your resilient spirit requires this field guide because, as Joe says, war is hell but life shouldn't be."

Eileen McDargh, CEO Chief Energy Officer, The Resiliency Group and author of *Your Resiliency GPS*

"*Winning the War with Yourself Field Manual* by Joe Tye is a timeless, thoughtful book written with zest and wisdom drawn from history, philosophy, psychology, Neuroscience, spirituality and personal experience. It is a must read for all who aspire to pre-eminence in their lives during their time on this beautiful earth."

Keerthy Sunder, M.D., Author of *Face your Addictions and Save your Life* and Creator of the Resiliency Challenge for PTSD

"Joe Tye provides a vital read for healthcare professionals in *The Winning the War with Yourself Field Manual*. Leading and influencing others with a positive approach is not possible unless we understand how to create positivity within ourselves. This excellent book provides the path and the tools for a daily focus on helping patients and co-workers by helping ourselves."

Nancy Schlichting: Chief Executive Officer, Henry Ford Health System and author of *Unconventional Leadership: What Henry Ford and Detroit Taught Me about Reinvention and Diversity*

"Do you ever find yourself doing things over and over and not getting to the outcomes that you hoped for? You want to change an aspect in your life or in the way you lead your organization but find that something is holding you back from doing it. In Joe Tye's *Winning the War with Yourself Field Manual* you will learn how to quickly identify those characteristics that define 'Your Own Worst Enemy' and then devise a plan on how to combat them. I found this to be an easy read manual that can be shared with executives at all levels in my organization. The principles described hit true to home and felt like they were being developed just for me. It's not just another flavor of the day program but a methodical approach to really looking inside of oneself and then making specific commitments that will help you control that 'Own Worst Enemy' that may have been preventing you in achieving the potential you know you have within. Get it! Share it! It will help you get out of your comfort zone and move you to a place that lets you realize your dreams and potential."

Ed Lamb, FACHE, President, Western Division, IASIS Healthcare and Chairman, American College of Healthcare Executives

"When Joe and I collaborated on my leadership book *Take the Stairs*, we talked a lot about the biggest barrier people face for achieving their goals as leaders and as sales professionals: overcoming self-limiting beliefs and self-sabotaging attitudes and behaviors. The strategies in this book will help you be a more effective leader, a more successful salesperson, and a better person. Joe shows you how to win the one war that you cannot afford to lose."

Roger Looyenga, Chairman and CEO (retired)
Auto-Owners Insurance Company

"If you want to stand out in a crowded world you must first stand up to the bully on the inside that wants you to sit down, shut up, and fit in. *Winning the War with Yourself Field Manual* will help you win the most important battle you will ever fight – the one that determines whether you win or lose in every other challenge you face."

Sam Horn, author of *Tongue Fu!* and *Got Your Attention?*

"As founder of BNI®, for more than 30 years I've had the opportunity to work with master networkers all over the world. One thing they all share in common is the ability to become masters of success by mastering themselves. They have learned how to overcome their own worst tendencies, to conquer fear and procrastination, and to make a genuine connection with other people. The strategies described in this book will help you to become a master of success, and a better person."

Ivan Misner, Founder and Chief Visionary Officer, BNI
and author of *The World's Best Known Marketing Secret*

"The principles and strategies outlined in this book have helped our people overcome some pretty significant inner enemies in their lives. We have seen people take charge of their health and lose weight, start work on long-postponed dreams including writing a book or starting a business, improve their relationships at work and at home, and most important be happier and more productive human beings. The Pickle Pledge, The Self Empowerment Pledge, The Twelve Core Action Values, and the other skills and strategies described in this book have truly transformed the lives of our people. This has translated into enhanced employee ownership, a better patient experience of care, and demonstrably better quality outcomes."

Bob Dent, Senior Vice President and COO/CNO Midland Memorial Hospital, Immediate Past Chair of the AONE Foundation, and author of "Promises" in *Chicken Soup for the Soul: Inspiration for Nurses*

"If you want to be inspired but too often fall into the trap of being Your Own Worst Enemy when dealing with life's adventures, tragedies, and disappointments then you must read *Winning the War with Yourself Field Manual*. In my opinion this is truly a classic written by a superbly talented writer who knows how important it is to face life head-on and not allow Your Own Worst Enemy to block your progress by undermining your self-discipline, sapping your psychic energy and eroding your sense of purpose. Joe Tye and the great commanders featured in this book give you all the weapons you need to defeat the worst enemy that is lurking in the dark shadows of your mind!"

Chuck Lauer, Publisher and Editorial Director (retired) of *Modern Healthcare* and author of *Soar with the Eagles, Reach for the Stars*, and *Decency*

"When it comes to winning the war with yourself, you couldn't ask for better teachers than Alexander the Great, Julius Caesar, Napoleon, Ulysses S. Grant, and the other masters of strategy Joe Tye has brought together in this book. A brilliant blending of history, psychology, and personal motivation that will inspire you to do more and be more."

Raymond Aaron, New York Times Bestselling Author

"In this book Joe Tye introduces you to your own worst enemy – yourself - and shows you how to win the battle against yourself to achieve a life of meaning and fulfilment. The timeless ideas in this book provide you with the battle armor you need to make your best future become reality."

Kevin Eikenberry, leadership expert and bestselling author of *Remarkable Leadership: Unleashing Your Leadership Potential One Skill at a Time*

CONTENTS

PART 3: THE SELF EMPOWERMENT PLEDGE

PART 4: THIS WAR IS NEVER OVER

A Note

to the Reader

Have you ever said or done something you later regretted? Found yourself putting off doing something that you really had to do or really wanted to do? Gone out on a binge of shopping therapy knowing that you were already behind on paying that month's bills? Heard yourself blaming someone else for problems that in your heart you knew you were causing all by your lonesome? Sat around complaining about problems rather than taking action to resolve them?

If your answer to any of these questions is no, then put this book down and immediately enroll yourself in a remedial course on honesty. If your answer is yes, then place your right hand in front of your face with palm out and thumb down, place your left hand in front of your face with palm in and thumb up, bring your two hands together – and shake hands with your own worst enemy. Meet YOWE – pronounced Yow-eee! Your Own Worst Enemy. The enemy within. YOWE is a greater threat to your future success and happiness than the toughest competitor, the most tyrannical boss, the most heartless creditor, the most disloyal friend or colleague, or any other enemy that's "out there."

In this book I will show you how to apply principles of warfare that have been used by history's most successful battlefield commanders to defeat this enemy within. Whatever goals you wish to achieve in your life, whatever person you want to make of yourself, YOWE is standing in your way and will use every weapon in its armamentarium to stop you. This book will give you the weapons you need to fight back – you must conquer the enemy "in here" before you can defeat any enemy that's "out there."

To study the strategies that made history's great commanders successful on the battlefield is not to justify the men themselves or the causes for which they fought. Alexander the Great, Genghis Khan, Napoleon Bonaparte, and their ilk were thugs, thieves, and murderers on a monstrous scale, worthy of condemnation, not admiration. As military historian John Keegan wrote of Alexander the Great (in his book *The Mask of Command*), "He destroyed much and created little or nothing... His dreadful legacy was to ennoble savagery in the name of glory and to leave a model of command that far too many men of ambition sought to act out in the centuries to come."

Still, there is no denying that these battlefield commanders were extraordinarily successful at defeating their enemies.

Military strategies themselves are neutral. They worked for George Washington the noble patriot as well as they did for Genghis Khan the vicious butcher. They will work for you in the ongoing war between you and YOWE.

If you don't use them, you can be sure that YOWE will use them against you.

How to use this book

Begin by reading Part 1 in its entirety. As Sun Tzu wrote in *The Art of War*, all military success begins with knowing the enemy – in this case YOWE. You will immediately recognize some of the weapons that YOWE uses against you, some others might surprise you (YOWE is a master of the sneak attack).

Part 2 includes seventy principles of military strategy organized in five sections. Some of them will reinforce things that you already know while others will be new, or at least presented in a new way. Many of these strategies reinforce one another. Some you will find immediately relevant to your current situation, others might sit on a mental shelf in the back of your head until you need them. Some you never will need.

If you have not done much study of military history, reading Part 2 might spark a new interest. The study of warfare illustrates human-kind at its most noble, courageous and enduring and at its cruelest, most cowardly and destructive. The history of warfare illustrates strategies brilliantly conceived and executed, and it illustrates what Barbara Tuchman called "the march of folly" in her masterful book of that title. And those lessons are all relevant to winning the war against YOWE, to achieving your most important goals, and for becoming the person you are meant to be.

In Part 3 we depart from the military theme – but this is by far the most important part of the book. The Self Empowerment Pledge features seven promises – one for each day of the week: Responsibility, Accountability, Determination, Contribution, Resilience, Perspective and Faith. Self empowerment is the antithesis of victimhood. It is the sword and shield you need in your fight to defeat YOWE. The truth is that no one can empower you but you yourself, and once you have empowered yourself no one can take that power from you.

Note: Throughout this book I refer to YOWE as it, not him or her. That's because, as real as its presence might feel, it is not part of the "him" or "her" that constitutes the real, authentic you. YOWE is like any other virus or parasite that exists solely to suck the life out of a host entity. And it is not your friend.

A Special Message to Executives

You have, I'm sure, heard the aphorism (coined by management guru Peter Drucker) that culture eats strategy for lunch. You've probably said it yourself. There are no doubt things you would like to see changed in the culture of your organization. But you have to understand that *culture does not change unless and until people change*, because at its core culture is a reflection of the collective attitudes, behaviors, and habits of the people who work there.

And you have to understand that people will not make and sustain personal change unless and until they conquer YOWE. The attitudes, behaviors, and habits that contribute to a negative culture are, without exception, a reflection of YOWE at work within the people who work there. Chronic complaining, incivility, bullying and lateral violence, learned helplessness and a "not my job" attitude are outward projections of negative self-talk, poor self-image, a victim mindset and the other mental manifestations of YOWE at work.

Culture does not change unless and until people change

That's why you should give a copy of this book to everyone in your organization – because the best investment you can make toward creating a better culture is an investment in helping your people be better people. And you will never build a culture of ownership in any organization where YOWE is allowed free rein in the way that people treat one another.

A SPECIAL MESSAGE TO HEALTHCARE PROFESSIONALS

There are two important reasons for you to read this book. First, as you well know, most of the people you care for need to take these lessons to heart. Why don't people quit smoking, lose weight, take their medications, take better care of themselves, and take the great advice you give them when they're in your hospital or clinic? There is one reason and one reason only: their best selves have waved the white flag of surrender to their lesser selves. You might well be able to help some of the patients you care for by sharing with them lessons from this book.

You cannot pour from an empty pitcher

The second reason is that many of your coworkers need these lessons – and to be quite honest there are probably days when you do as well. The healthcare literature overflows with articles about burnout, bullying, lateral violence, and other manifestations of people's lesser selves at work. We often ask "Who cares for the caregiver?" The answer is that we need to care for ourselves and we need to care for each other. And that caring begins with winning the war with our lesser selves.

A SPECIAL MESSAGE TO SALES PROFESSIONALS

You know better than anyone just how harmful YOWE can be to your career. Every fear that prevents you from doing the work that must be done if you are to achieve your goals is a reflection of YOWE at work.

You must win the war with yourself before you can prevail in the marketplace

To achieve a successful career in any sales position you must make that all-important first sale: selling you on you. And YOWE will use every weapon in its arsenal – including fear of rejection, low self-esteem, and complacency – to prevent you from making that sale.

A SPECIAL MESSAGE TO PARENTS

When I teach classes on values-based life and leadership skills, I am always impressed by the way people are taking notes and by the insights they describe during and after the sessions. But it always raises this question in the back of my mind: If they are just now learning about these skills and having these insights, then who's been teaching them to their children? I cannot strongly enough encourage you to share what you learn from this book with your kids. I guarantee you that – especially with today's emphasis on science, technology, math and with teachers whose idea of a great student is someone who will sit down, shut up, and soak it in, no one is teaching your children the essential skills of  emotional intelligence and mental toughness that are so essential to surviving and thriving in today's turbulent, uncertain, and hypercompetitive world.

A Special Message to Teens

The most frequent comment I've heard from people who reviewed early manuscripts of this book has been some variation of "I wish I'd known these things when I was in school." I say the same thing myself. I hope this book will help prevent you from someday saying the same thing by helping you avoid the pitfalls that are inevitable when your lesser self is calling the shots.

Unfortunately – and sometimes tragically – it is precisely during teen years that what I refer to as YOWE (Your Own Worst Enemy) can have the most horrific impact on your life. Drunk driving, drug addiction, unwanted pregnancy and many other bad things can happen when your lesser self takes the wheel. Sometimes with consequences that you will regret for the rest of your life.

Someday you will wish that you'd learned all this sooner

So I hope this book will help you recognize the weapons that your inner enemy will use against you, and learn how to combat them. If you don't pay attention to it now, then it's a safe bet that someday you too will be saying that you wish you'd learned all of this stuff sooner.

A SPECIAL MESSAGE TO VETERANS OF MILITARY SERVICE

I especially hope that you will find this book helpful. Reading stories of great victories, inspired leadership when everything's on the line, and courageous stands in the face of tough odds will, I hope, remind you of the reasons you joined the armed forces and of the lessons you learned during your time there.

But even more so, I hope this book will be a helpful resource for those of you who have suffered physical, psychological and emotional injuries as a result of your service. In his book *War and the Soul: Healing Our Nation's Veterans from Post-Traumatic Stress Disorder*, Dr. Edward Tick wrote that PTSD is not a stress disorder so much as it is an identity disorder. When you allow your sense of identity to be defined by old wounds, you are playing into the hands of Your Own Worst Enemy,  which I call YOWE. As you will see in this book, YOWE wants to hold you in a permanent victim mindset, feeling sorry for yourself and seeking pity from others. The essential first step to reclaiming your authentic identity is to subjugate YOWE. This book will show you how.

PART 1

YOWE – Your Own Worst Enemy

*To win any of the other wars of life you must first
win the war with yourself.*

MEET YOWE – YOUR OWN WORST ENEMY

"I have met the enemy and it's me."

(with thanks to John Paul Jones and Pogo)

I'm sure you've seen pictures depicting a man or woman with an angel on one shoulder and a devil on the other shoulder. The image represents the age-old inner conflict between your ideal best self and the lesser self that causes you to self-sabotage the dreams and ideals of that best self. That is the nature of being human.

Daniel Goleman has done more than anyone to popularize research on emotional intelligence*. When it comes to career and personal success and achievement, he says, one's EQ is far more important than their IQ. Unfortunately, as the human brain has evolved the incredible abilities that created the world we live in it is still saddled with the proverbial lizard brain. Any time you have a temper tantrum, a panic attack, or other form of what Goleman calls an emotional hijacking, you know that lizard brain has commandeered your mental ship. And YOWE is calling the shots.

Before engaging with any enemy, the military commander must have a thorough knowledge of the weapons that enemy is able to bring to the fight so he can counter them. The same is true for your battle with YOWE. You will know you are under attack by YOWE any time:

» You hear the voice of negative self-talk telling you that you're not good enough, not smart enough, not tough enough, not pretty enough, too old or not old enough, and that you don't deserve to realize your most cherished goals and dreams because you're just – well, you're just you.

» You start on a new project, venture, or calling with great enthusiasm, but then throw in the towel upon hitting the first bump in the road.

» You've been working on a project, venture, or calling with great determination and dedication but then seem to run out of gas just before the point where you could otherwise have achieved a significant breakthrough.

» You care more about what you think other people might think of you than you care about what you think of yourself.

» You blame circumstances, history, other people or any other outside factor for your problems rather than accepting complete personal responsibility for them.

» You whine, complain, or otherwise play the role of victim or martyr instead of being grateful for the blessings of your life and being determined to plow through the barriers that stand between you and achieving your future goals.

» You waste time and energy criticizing, ridiculing, or demeaning other people instead of working to strengthen your own character and develop your own talents and skills.

» You allow yourself to fall into a state of anxiety or depression without doing everything within your power to fight your way back to a more positive emotional state.

» You turn on the TV or mindlessly check email and surf the web while important work sits unattended and undone.

» There is a significant gap between what you say your values are and what the proverbial Man from Mars would see recorded in your calendar and your checkbook register.

» You wait for someone else to give you permission – to "empower" you – to achieve your goals and be your best self rather than claiming your power and giving yourself the permission you need to make a commitment and take action.

» In any other way that you engage in self-sabotaging attitudes or behaviors.

YOWE declared war on the authentic and brilliant person you were meant to be the first time you heard the word NO. Sometimes YOWE will mount a full scale frontal assault, and at other times use guerilla tactics to defeat you, but it will never stop. YOWE will throw up brick walls when you're on a roll, and kick you when you're flat on your back.

Have you seen the picture of the tabby cat looking in a mirror and seeing a lion looking back? That lion in the mirror is the person you are meant-to-be. And YOWE is the only thing preventing the tabby cat from becoming the lion.

Defeating YOWE is the essential first step toward winning in life.

---

* Goleman's books on the subject include *Emotional Intelligence, Working with Emotional Intelligence,* and *Primal Leadership.*

THE TRIPPING POINT

Several years ago, Malcolm Gladwell's book *The Tipping Point* described how small things can add up to make a big difference. For many of us, however, a more relevant title would be *The Tripping Point*, about how seemingly minor deficiencies in character, attitudes, behaviors, and habits can accumulate to trip you up and prevent you from achieving your personal, professional, and financial goals and, in the worst case, bring about catastrophic failure on all of these fronts. How that tripping point can cause you to be defeated by YOWE.

YOWE is comprised of self-restricting beliefs that prevent us from experiencing the adventure of leaving our comfort zones; negative attitudes that focus our attention on risk and scarcity instead of opportunity and abundance; poor habits that cause procrastination and disorganization; lack of emotional control that provokes us to say and do things we later regret; and all of the other ways in which inner beliefs, attitudes, and behaviors prevent us from realizing our dreams and fulfilling our potential.

Whether you realize it or not, you are in a lifelong war with YOWE. You will win some battles and you will lose some battles; there will be periods of intense fighting and times when a tenuous truce prevails; sometimes you will hold your sword to YOWE's throat and at other times you will waive the white flag of surrender and give in to the demands of the lesser self that YOWE represents. But make no mistake, the war will go on until the day you die. How effectively you wage that war will determine the goals you achieve (or fail to achieve), the quality of your relationships with others, and the contributions you make (or don't make) to making your corner of the world a better place. It will determine the nature of the person you see looking back at you from the mirror every morning and whether you live your life striving to be your authentic best self or settle for being a second-rate shadow of that best self.

The Bible asks who would light a candle and then put a basket over it. We all have that candle burning inside of us. It is the authentic, meant to be best self that wants to do work that matters, that wants to be passionate and pursue life with courage and determination, and that wants to make a difference in the world. The one and only purpose of YOWE is to put a basket over that candle and hold it there until the light is extinguished. Your best self wants to play the game in the real world – YOWE wants you to watch someone else play the game on reality TV.

In his book *Cool, Hip and Sober: 88 Ways to Beat Booze and Drugs* Bill Manville writes about his realization that what he thought of as his "secret friend" – the inner presence he satisfied with his drinking – was really an enemy that wanted to kill him. He had finally seen that his favorite drink-

Every time you defeat YOWE you become stronger and move closer to your goals.

ing buddy was really YOWE, and that YOWE would rather see him dead than sober. I'm sure you've seen images of the man or woman who has an angel on one shoulder and a devil on the other shoulder. The angel is your meant-to-be best self. The devil is YOWE.

The stakes are enormous. Every time you defeat YOWE you become a stronger and better person and move closer to the achievement of your most important goals and dreams. Every time YOWE defeats you, you settle for anemic dreams and goals and a little bit more of your authentic best self dies. Since this is a war, it behooves you to study the strategies by which history's greatest commanders achieved their victories.

YOWE's Weapons in the War against Your Best Self

When it comes to winning the war against YOWE you are unfortunately at a disadvantage. Many of the weapons you were born with have grown weaker over time. When you were a little kid you had the insatiable curiosity of The Elephant's Child. You weren't afraid to ask "why?" without ever worrying whether or not it was a dumb question. You had big dreams for yourself: you were going to be Superman or an astronaut, not sit in a dark cubicle doing spreadsheets while dreading the day you'd be summoned to the HR office and given a pink slip. You weren't afraid to skip down the hallways because it never even dawned on you to care about what other people thought of you. You could sing, you could dance, you could make art and write poetry, and you didn't need to have someone else validate your performance because that's not why you were doing it.

But over the years you ran into parents, teachers, schoolyard bullies, and eventually abusive bosses and toxic coworkers. Gradually, almost imperceptibly, the basket began to be lowered over your candle. The lion you once saw looking back at you from the mirror morphed into an alley cat, and once magnificent dreams transmogrified into fantasies and daydreams.

At the same time all this was happening, YOWE was insidiously growing stronger. Like Hitler's Germany secretly rearming between the two world wars, during your adolescent years YOWE was developing and refining the weapons with which to prevent you from becoming your authentic best self and achieving your most important goals in life. These weapons include:

» *Negative self-talk:* This is the toxic voice of YOWE telling you that you're not good enough, not smart enough, not pretty enough. Negative self-talk is YOWE telling you lies – and then you falling for those lies. Of course, by embracing the lies you ultimately make them your reality. Believing that you are not good enough, smart enough, or pretty enough will make it so.

» *Low self-esteem:* Low self-esteem is often nothing more than an excuse for cowardice and laziness. People with low self-esteem don't have the courage to ask because they're afraid they'll be rejected, and they don't have the gumption to try because they're afraid they'll fail.

» *Poor self-image:* YOWE causes you to look at yourself as through a fun house mirror that magnifies your weaknesses and diminishes your strengths. You will never on a sustained basis exceed the potential of the person you see looking back at you from the mirror. If you see yourself as a winner, no obstacle or setback will prevent you from doing whatever it takes for you to achieve the goals needed to bring together your inner and outer realities. On the other hand, if you see yourself as a victim or a loser, no windfall gain will prevent you from acting in ways that cause you to self-sabotage your victory so as to make your outer reality coincide with your inner image of yourself.

» *Invidious comparison:* One of YOWE's most effective ways of putting you down is comparing you to others in such a way as to make sure that you come out on the short end of the comparison. The biggest problem with such invidious comparisons is that YOWE will always compare you at your worst against someone else at their best. When a man sees Arnold Schwarzenegger on a magazine cover in the checkout line, YOWE stacks him up against The Terminator's biceps and bank account, not against his parenting prowess.

» *Concern for appearances:* YOWE won't let you skip down the corridors where you work, sing karaoke at the bar, write bad poetry and draw childish pictures because it's got you scared to death imagining what other people – including total strangers – might think. YOWE will look the other way as you choke down a gooey cinnamon bun and slurp on a supersized latte overflowing with whipped cream at the airport terminal, but start doing pushups by the window and it will mount a full-scale frontal assault to make you sit down, shut up, and not stand out (echoing words that you have been hearing since you were a toddler).

» *Self-pity:* Any time you catch yourself whining and complaining about something – anything at all – you have fallen victim to one of YOWE's most potent weapons. Playing victim or martyr when things don't go your way is YOWE's way of keeping you from holding yourself responsible and accountable for your life, being determined to achieve your goals, and being resilient in the face of adversity.

» *Blaming others:* Legendary basketball coach John Wooden said that whether you win or lose a game, you're never a loser until you start to blame someone else for the loss. Finger-pointing and passing the buck is a reflection of your lesser self. Any time you catch yourself blaming someone else for your problems, you can be sure that YOWE is behind the curtain pulling the strings.

» *Self-sabotage:* In his indispensable book *The War of Art*, Steve Pressfield calls the fear of success "the mother of all fears" and says that the closer one comes to achieving a goal the more fierce will be the Resistance (he capitalizes the word Resistance the way historians capitalize Black Plague and Great Depression). YOWE knows that every time you prevail you get stronger, so the closer you come to victory the more frantically it will fight you. Thomas Edison said that people would be appalled if they knew how close to success they were when they quit. YOWE wants to make sure that you never know how close you are and loves nothing better than to cause you to snatch defeat from the jaws of victory.

Self-awareness begins with recognizing the weapons YOWE uses to prevent you from being your best self

TOXIC EMOTIONAL NEGATIVITY IS MALIGNANT

If you read *The Iliad* by Homer (or saw the movie *Troy*) you recall the scene where Achilles – mightiest of the Greek warriors – sulked in his tent and refused to come out and fight even as his countrymen were suffering defeat on the field of battle. His sulk ended costing the life of his dearest friend Patroclus.

That is a great metaphor for the damage that toxic emotional negativity can impose on the emotional vampire (another great metaphor) his or herself, the people around him or her, and the entire organization.

The first step to creating a more positive workplace culture is often fostering a higher level of intolerance for toxic emotional negativity, as reflected in chronic complaining, gossiping, and passive-aggressive behavior. In his pioneering work on emotional intelligence, Daniel Goleman shows how one toxically negative person can drag down the morale and productivity of an entire work unit. Teaching people practical skills to confront bullying, gossip and rumor-mongering, and chronic complaining in a positive and constructive manner is an essential investment in a more positive workplace environment.

Toxic emotional negativity is the emotional and spiritual equivalent of cigarette smoke – malignant and contagious.

In a very real sense, toxic emotional negativity is the emotional and spiritual equivalent of cigarette smoke. It is malignantly harmful to the person who is afflicted with it, and is a contagion that will infect everyone else upon whom it is inflicted.

In fact, the science is now so clear and definitive that a very strong case can be made that toxic emotional negativity (TEN) should be designated as a disease category just like cancer or heart disease.

Any time you give in to negative attitudes, any time you wallow around in toxic emotional negativity, you can be quite certain that YOWE is behind the curtain pulling the strings.

TOXIC EMOTIONAL NEGATIVITY IS CONTAGIOUS

"Panic gathers volume like a snowball… Nothing is more likely to collapse a line of infantry than the sight of a few of its members in full and unexplained flight. Precipitate movement in the wrong direction is an open invitation to disaster."

S.L.A. Marshall: Men Against Fire

Toxic emotional negativity is as contagious as flu bug in a kindergarten class. Just as one person lighting a cigarette in a closed room instantly pollutes the lungs of everyone else in that room, so too one emotional vampire can suck the life out of an entire department of the organization. YOWE will enlist these nattering nabobs of negativity (Spiro Agnew's one enduring contribution to the lexicon) into the fight to prevent you from doing your best and being your best.

I learned this exercise from my good friend Roger Looyenga, retired CEO of the Auto-Owners Insurance Company. Roger would stand in front of a classroom and hold up two glass coffee mugs, one half full with clear water and the other half full with black coffee. He would take a spoonful of water from that cup and pour it into the coffee, then ask his audience what changed. The answer, of course, was nothing – the coffee was still as black as it had been before the spoonful of water had been poured into it. Then he would pour a spoonful of coffee into the water, which of course instantly discolored.

As Roger would point out, it's the same thing with people. If one truly positive person is placed in a toxic negative workplace environment, they will either leave, withdraw into themselves, or gradually and insidiously become more toxically negative themselves. On the other hand, one toxic negative person injected into a positive work unit can pollute the emotional environment of an entire workplace.

Here's what I said about the leadership obligation to eradicate toxic emotional negativity from the workplace in my book *The Florence Prescription: From Accountability to Ownership*:

> One toxically negative person can drag down the morale and the productivity of an entire work unit. It is a core leadership responsibility to create a workplace where toxic emotional negativity is not tolerated.

> It takes courage to stand up to the bully, the emotional vampire, and the cynical pickle sucker, but that is the duty of anyone who presumes to be a leader. It is your obligation as a leader to protect the people for whom (and to whom) you are responsible from the baleful effects of the people who – through their toxic attitudes and destructive behaviors – poison the emotional climate of the workplace.

HOW YOWE ABUSES YOUR IMAGINATION

"There is no victory in any war except through our imaginations."

Dwight D. Eisenhower

"Vision is the art of seeing the invisible."

Jonathon Swift

Imagination is a God-given gift that only we humans have been blessed with. Only humans can, to paraphrase the memorable words of Antoine de Saint-Exupéry (author of *The Little Prince* whose fighter plane disappeared over the Mediterranean while on a mission during World War II), look at a rock pile and see a cathedral. Dolphins cannot blueprint a city, dogs cannot plan a career, and no parakeet ever imagined a new technology. Imagination is what gives us the power to create a new vision.

Without vision people perish, Proverbs tells us. That is the goal of YOWE. It knows that the more powerful and beautiful your vision for the future, the stronger your best self becomes and the weaker YOWE becomes. YOWE cannot destroy your imagination – that power is too deeply ingrained in your DNA. But it can do something far worse – it can warp imagination to its own purposes and use it as a weapon against your best self.

YOWE abuses your imagination in two ways. The first is worry. To worry is to imagine something bad happening in your future. YOWE loves it when you waste your time and emotional energy with toxic worry – it makes you feel like you are the center of the universe (you must really be important to have so many worries). Worry can be useful if it galvanizes you to take effective action to prevent whatever it is you're worried about from happening, but YOWE will crank it up to such a toxic level that you become paralyzed. A fundamental precept of military strategy is that when you deprive an enemy of mobility you have placed him at a grave disadvantage. YOWE wants to see your best self immobilized by worry.

The second way YOWE abuses your imagination is fantasy – imagining a beautiful future that you have no intention of working to create. Again, a little fantasy can be a good thing if it inspires you with a dream, if it inspires you to take a risk and to take action. But fantasy without commitment to doing the work is the mental equivalent of watching someone else on a "reality" TV show rather than working to create a new reality of your own.

YOWE uses worry and fantasy as a one-two punch to prevent you from taking productive action to achieve your biggest, most important goals. First it paralyzes you with toxic worry: "What if I invest all the time to write a book and then nobody buys it?"

Then, to prevent you from summoning up the courage to actually start writing, it sedates you with fantasy: you imagine yourself chatting with J.K. Rowling and John Grisham on the deck of a cruise ship, periodically being interrupted by adoring fans begging for your autograph. And before you know it your dream has withered into just another meaningless daydream.

> Focus your imagination on constructive dreams; don't let YOWE abuse it with worry and fantasy.

YOWE loves it when you waste your time on meaningless daydreams. They give ego the same feel-good rush as the real thing without having to suffer the inconvenience of doing the work required to make the real thing happen.

YOWE AND THE ANATOMY OF FAILURE

In their book *Military Misfortune: The Anatomy of Failure in War*, Eliot A. Cohen and John Gooch state that there are three kinds of failure in warfare – failure to learn, failure to anticipate, and failure to adapt to changing circumstances. "Where learning failures have their roots in the past, and anticipating failures look to the future, adaptive failures suggest an inability to handle the changing present." When all three forms of failure occur together, they say, the result is a perfect storm of catastrophic disaster. They cite the collapse of the French military under the weight of German *Blitzkrieg* in the spring of 1940 as one such perfect storm.

YOWE will cause personal misfortune and failure in the same three ways:

» *YOWE never learns.* YOWE makes the same mistake over and over, each time expecting that somehow, magically, a different outcome will ensue (Albert Einstein's definition of insanity). YOWE asks the same questions over and over, each time expecting that somehow – without you having done anything to change circumstances – you will receive a different answer.

» *YOWE never anticipates.* YOWE lives for instant gratification (and complains that even that takes too long), and feels no responsibility whatsoever for the health, wealth, and welfare of the person you will be in the future because it refuses to see beyond the horizons of today's desires.

» *YOWE never adapts.* Its response to losing a job isn't learning new skills, moving into a new profession, or starting a new business – its response is to mindlessly seek another job doing the same thing you were doing in the old job. YOWE never adapts because that would mean taking risk, leaving the sanctuary of the old "comfort zone," and actually facing your fears instead of running away from them.

If you let YOWE call the shots in your life by refusing to learn, refusing to anticipate, and refusing to adapt, you too run the risk of setting yourself up for catastrophic failure.

Failure to learn, to anticipate, and to adapt create a perfect storm of failure

You Will Have to Swim Against the Current

Unfortunately, to conquer YOWE requires that you swim against a strong cultural current that is going in the wrong direction. The more affluent, comfortable, convenient and secure our society becomes, it seems, the more addicted we become to mindless self-indulgence. For example:

» The average American watches between three and five hours of television per day – and that is over and above time spent surfing the web, texting and twittering friends and strangers, and taking selfie photos.

» The average American reads only 6 books a year, and nearly one out of four doesn't read a single book – and these figures include trashy romance novels, not just great literature and other books that nourish the mind, heart, and spirit.

» The American Dream was once to work hard, build a career or start a business, and own a home. The new American Dream is to win the lottery. Lottery ticket sales appear to be one of the few recession-proof consumer goods. In 2012, Americans blew $78 billion (yes, that's billion with a B) on lottery tickets in the hopes that Uncle Lotto would give them money that they didn't have to work to earn, and that they don't deserve, because they don't have the gumption to go out and earn it themselves.

» On top of money wasted on lottery tickets, casinos are sprouting up across America like mushrooms in a dark wood after a big storm. In 2012, Americans blew $37 billion (again, billion with a B) gambling in casinos. While for many older people this is their idea of a dream "retirement" (re-tire – to get tired again), gambling addiction is increasingly prevalent in younger age groups. According to a report from the Association of Gaming Equipment Manufacturers, young adults (21-35) have the highest rate of casino visitation and report the highest likelihood of making a return visit to the tables and the slots.

» More than 35% of Americans are obese. According to the USDA, the average American consumed almost 20% more calories in the year 2000 than they did in 1983 – and it has almost certainly gone up since then. Paradoxically, Americans spend more than $20 billion per year  on weight loss schemes, often in the hopes that they can somehow magically produce a svelte figure with 6-pack abs without having to give up 6 packs, supersized fast food meals, or ever darken the threshold of a workout studio.

Every time you give into mindless self-indulgence, you let YOWE win another little victory against your best self.

It takes courage to go against the current when YOWE is standing there on the river bank ready to give you an umbrella drink and plop you down in a rubber ducky raft, and then to push you out on that current of mindless self-indulgence as your life slips away, one lazy day after another.

DRAW YOUR LINE IN THE SAND

Legend has it that on the day before the Alamo fell to the Mexican army, leaving no survivors, Commander William Barrett Travis called his ragtag band of Texians (that's what they called themselves before they were Texans and Americans) into the courtyard of their surrounded compound. He told them that the final Mexican assault would come soon, and that no outside help was on the way. He then drew a long deep line in the sand and said, "I now want every man who is determined to stay here and die with me to come across this line. Who will be the first?" Virtually to a man they stepped cross, and to a man over the next two days they did indeed die with their commander. Some months after the battle a young man named J. Frank Dobie visited the Alamo and went to the place where Travis had drawn his

Your biggest dreams lie on the other side of that line in the sand.

line in the sand. "Nobody forgets the line," he wrote. "It is drawn too deep and straight." *

You cannot see YOWE the way Travis and his men could see Mexican General Santa Ana's army surrounding them at the Alamo. But you can feel its presence. Every time you say or do something you know you'll later regret, every time you back down from fear and give up on a dream, every time you put off doing important work, every time you look in the mirror and pretend to see in the person looking back at you less than the person you are capable of being, you have been defeated by this enemy.

You are in a fight to the death with YOWE. It's a fight you can win. It's a fight you *must* win if you are to achieve your most important goals in life and to become the person you are meant to be. This book is your battle plan for winning the war with yourself. We'll draw upon strategies devised by the greatest military commanders in history to help you combat and ultimately defeat YOWE. But you must draw your line in the sand.

Will you draw that line in the sand, making it as deep and straight as the one Colonel Travis scratched into the dirt of the Alamo court-yard? Will you step across that line, declaring your independence from YOWE and your determination to fight for the freedom to be the person you were meant to be?

If your answer is yes, pick up your sword and turn the page.

* Louis Moses Rose was the one man who did not step across the line and who escaped the day before the final assault – it is to him that we owe knowledge of the story of the line drawn by Colonel Travis (as recounted in Lon Tinkle's book *Thirteen Days to Glory: The Siege of the Alamo*).

PART 2

APPLYING THE
PRINCIPLES OF
MILITARY STRATEGY

*The greatest triumph of the human spirit is to successfully
become the person you were meant to be. The greatest tragedy is to
successfully pretend to be someone else.*

DEFINE YOUR CORE VALUES

In *Hope is Not a Method: What Business Leaders Can Learn from America's Army*, Gordon R. Sullivan and Michael V. Harper wrote: "One of the most important lessons we learned during the rebuilding of the Army after Vietnam was the importance of values – a commitment by all soldiers to something larger than themselves." Core values are deeply-held philosophical guideposts that define how you think, how you act, how you set goals and priorities, how you build relationships, and how you manage conflict. Your core values should define who you are, what you stand for, and what you won't stand for. But unless acted upon, core values are nothing more than good intentions (and you know what they say about the road to hell!).

Defining your personal values, and the attitudes, behaviors and habits dictated by those values, is one of the most important and empowering exercises you will ever undertake.

Since you're reading this book, I'm confident in saying that you intuitively have good solid values. But I'm also fairly certain that you've never taken the time to write them down, much less prioritize them; that you've never done an audit of your calendar and checkbook register to see how the decisions you make with regard to spending time and money comport with the values you claim to hold; that you've never explicitly defined how those values guide your relationships and how you deal with conflict; and that you've never thought through how you would make a decision if you could honor one important value or another but not both.

The catastrophic collapse of Enron was caused in large part by the fact that thousands of people who knew what was going on were forced to choose between the values of loyalty and honesty. At Enron to be loyal meant to be dishonest, to look the other way at the unethical behavior going on all around. And to be honest meant to be disloyal, and to know that there would be a price to be paid for speaking out. Almost to a person Enron employees chose to be loyal to the company rather than to be honest with themselves.

At Values Coach we teach a course on values-based life and leadership skills called *The Twelve Core Action Values*. It's a 60-module course built around twelve values that are universal and eternal – no matter your politics, religious belief or non-belief, ethnic heritage, socioeconomic background, or any other factor, from Authenticity to Leadership these are values that you aspire to live. Each value is reinforced by four cornerstones that put action into the values.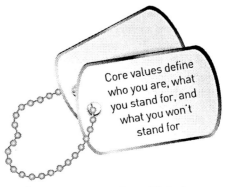
Take a look at the course outline on the next page. It will help you think more clearly about what your core values are, and about the commitments to action that those values entail.

For more on The Twelve Core Action Values and to download the free *360-Day Personal Journal* go to www.ValuesCoach.com/values.

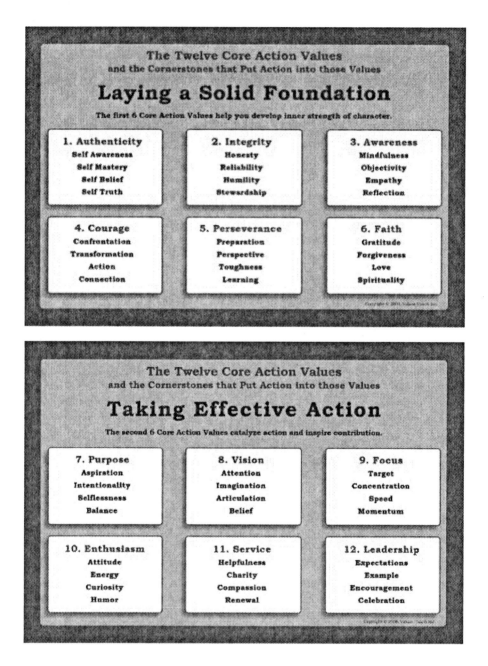

The Twelve Core Action Values
and the Cornerstones that Put Action into those Values

Laying a Solid Foundation

The first 6 Core Action Values help you develop inner strength of character.

1. Authenticity
Self Awareness
Self Mastery
Self Belief
Self Truth

2. Integrity
Honesty
Reliability
Humility
Stewardship

3. Awareness
Mindfulness
Objectivity
Empathy
Reflection

4. Courage
Confrontation
Transformation
Action
Connection

5. Perseverance
Preparation
Perspective
Toughness
Learning

6. Faith
Gratitude
Forgiveness
Love
Spirituality

The Twelve Core Action Values
and the Cornerstones that Put Action into those Values

Taking Effective Action

The second 6 Core Action Values catalyze action and inspire contribution.

7. Purpose
Aspiration
Intentionality
Selflessness
Balance

8. Vision
Attention
Imagination
Articulation
Belief

9. Focus
Target
Concentration
Speed
Momentum

10. Enthusiasm
Attitude
Energy
Curiosity
Humor

11. Service
Helpfulness
Charity
Compassion
Renewal

12. Leadership
Expectations
Example
Encouragement
Celebration

STICK TO YOUR PRINCIPLES

In his speech accepting the 1953 Nobel Peace Prize General George C. Marshall said, "Discouraged people are in sore need of great principles." Principles build upon values by defining concordant attitudes and behaviors. For example, I'm confident that one of the core values you aspire to is integrity. Because talking about another person behind that person's back is without exception disrespectful and dishonest, it is a principle of integrity that one should never engage in gossip and rumor-mongering. Being involved in a gossip session, even as a passive listener, violates the dignity of the gossipee and the integrity of the gossiper.

In a paradox we'll see repeatedly, it's easy to stick to your principles when there is no temptation to violate them. It's after you've lost a job, been passed over for a promotion, been threatened with foreclosure by your bank, received bad news from your doctor, suffered heartbreak, or otherwise experienced a serious setback or disappointment that you most need to be guided by great principles. And  it is precisely at those discouraging moments when it is most difficult.

In his classic text *On War*, Carl von Clausewitz wrote about the difficulties of perceiving things correctly when one is enshrouded in what he called "the fog of war." That's a great metaphor for the challenge of holding to your principles when it feels like YOWE has you surrounded and outgunned. If you wait until the setback or disappointment has occurred to define your principles, it's likely to be too late to act upon them.

It takes courage to stand up and walk away when the rumor mill starts to grind, especially if you desperately want to feel included in the group. It's in such times of temptation that you are "in sore need of great principles."

Choose to Do Work that Really Matters

Nobody gave Joan of Arc the job of leading the hitherto battered French army on to victory against the English invaders at Orleans; Florence Nightingale did not receive paychecks or performance appraisals for her work improving the quality of army field hospitals during the Crimean War; Clara Barton – the "Angel of the Battlefield" during the American Civil War – did not go on to found the American Red Cross for personal fame and fortune. Yet each of these women had

a greater impact on the world, and are better remembered by history, than most of the generals who led the armies with which they were associated. Here are several questions that can help you think about the work you choose to do:

What work would your best self choose to do?

- » What would you do if every job paid the same and had the same social status?

- » What would you do if you knew you could not fail?

- » What would you do if you weren't afraid? (A favorite question of my friend Traci Fenton, founder of WorldBlu.)

- » What would you do if you stopped worrying about what other people might think of you?

- » What would you do if you had only one more year to live?

» What would you do if you knew you were going to live to be 110 years old?

» Imagine that ten years from now you won the Nobel Prize (or the Pulitzer Prize or whatever other prize suits your fancy or fantasy). What was it for?

» What one thing would you like to know that your great grandchildren will be told about you?

What are the implications of your answers? What would you be doing differently tomorrow if you were to act upon those answers today?

COMMIT YOURSELF TO A CAUSE THAT TRANSCENDS SELF-INTEREST

"Someone with a job is never secure; someone with a calling is never unemployed."

McZen

Hannibal is remembered as one of history's greatest battlefield generals, but he ultimately failed in his war against Rome in large part because he lacked an overarching sense of purpose or mission. He beat the Romans in battle after battle, but never really had a goal beyond beating the Romans in battle. Largely as a result, he ended up winning the big battles but losing the war, and in the end seeing his army defeated and his city of Carthage obliterated.

In *Why the Allies Won*, Richard Overy wrote that the belief they were fighting for a righteous cause "gave a genuine moral certainty to the Allies, which the Axis populations largely lacked." This sense of purpose, he wrote, was every bit as important as material resources, military strategy, and fighting skills in explaining the outcome of the war.

Being devoted to a cause that transcends self-interest will help you attack life with a spirit of commitment and adventure, and better withstand the inevitable barbs and slings of the tough world you will encounter when you do. People did not march with Martin Luther King because they wanted to take a walk, people do not help Habitat for Humanity build houses because they like to pound nails, and young college graduates don't join Teach for America because they want a low-paid sabbatical at an inner city school. The acid test of leadership, including self-leadership, is the ability to create a sense of transcendent meaning and purpose to the work itself.

YOWE's antennae are eternally tuned to radio station WIIFM — What's In It For Me? When you commit your time and energy to a cause that transcends your own needs and wants but rather is devoted to helping other people and to making your corner of the world a better place, YOWE is cut completely out of the picture. It will yell and squall like a spoiled little brat who didn't get what it wanted for

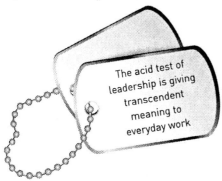

The acid test of leadership is giving transcendent meaning to everyday work

Christmas, but if you tune the squealing out you will hear the soft voice of your best self giving you guidance, and begin to achieve the sort of emotional equanimity and spiritual peace that are Kryptonite to YOWE.

Know What You Want

In *On Strategy: A Critical Analysis of the Vietnam War*, Harry G. Summers wrote that nearly 70 percent of the generals who participated in that war were uncertain of our objectives, which "had a devastating effect on our ability to conduct the war." More recently, the first Iraq War is remembered as a military success largely because the objective was crystal clear (throwing the Iraqi invaders out of Kuwait, then coming home). The second Iraq War, on the other hand, will be remembered at best as a stalemated quagmire and at worst as a complete fiasco (*Fiasco* is the title of a book about that war by author Thomas Ricks) largely because the objectives were muddy almost from the very beginning: Was the war launched because of weapons of mass destruction (real or imagined)? Was it about fighting terrorism? Ridding the world of an evil dictator? Grabbing control of future oil supplies? Padding the coffers of Halliburton or any of the other more sinister motives ascribed by the war's most vociferous critics? We still don't know for sure and probably never will.

The same is true when it comes to winning the war with yourself. The more clear you are about what you want, the more effectively you will use your time and your energy. And the more capable you will be of saying no to all the distractions, diversions, detours, and bright shiny objects that YOWE throws in front of you in the attempt to prevent you from concentrating your energy and effort on the one thing that matters most.

"What do you want?" is a deceptively and often devilishly difficult question to answer. I know this from personal experience. I spent 20 years convinced that what I really wanted was to be CEO of a big teaching hospital. Only after I was let go from my last position as chief operating officer of one such hospital did I give myself permission to ask that life-changing question: "What would you do if every job paid the same and had the same social status?" My answer to that question took me in a completely different direction from the one I'd been pursuing the previous two decades and led to the founding of Values Coach, and eventually to the writing of this book.

One more thing: If you were to read every book that's ever been written and listen to every audio program that's ever been recorded on the subject of setting and achieving goals, you'd get lots of different sorts of advice, but virtually every authority would agree upon this one thing: the best way to assure that you will achieve your goals is to write them down as clearly as you can and post them where you will see them often. You need to keep reminding yourself of what it is you really want.

KNOW HOW YOU'RE GOING TO GET IT

In *Military Blunders: The How and Why of Military Failure* Saul David wrote: "Perhaps the least forgivable of all military blunders are those committed at the planning stage. For they often condemn the soldiers involved – officers and men alike – to certain defeat before the battle has even begun." You've probably heard that failing to plan is planning to fail. And you've probably also heard that most people will devote more time and energy to planning a vacation than they do to planning the rest of their career or planning for their retirement.

That is the work of YOWE. YOWE wants to live in the moment, play it by ear, go with the flow, take it easy and take it as it comes. YOWE knows that planning is hard work now that entails even more hard work later; as management guru Peter Drucker reminded us, even the most beautiful of plans must eventually degenerate into work. If your plan is to earn a graduate nursing degree or start a business, YOWE knows you will not accomplish that goal by watching General Hospital or Shark Tank on TV. You're going to have to learn new things (YOWE hates to study), make sacrifices to be able to better focus your time and money (YOWE hates self-sacrifice), and take some risk (YOWE wants to keep you firmly seated on the sofa of your comfort zone). Furthermore, creating a plan is an act of accepting responsibility – it spells out the actions you must take in order to achieve your stated goals; YOWE would much rather take it one day at a time and then blame everyone else when the ultimate day of reckoning ends up being unpleasant.

Creating a plan of attack is one of your most powerful weapons for subduing YOWE. When you have a plan and a commitment to stick with it, making adjustments as necessary, you define priorities and close the door to distractions. You create structure. YOWE hates structure and would rather have the faux-structure of knowing that tomorrow will be a lot like yesterday was.

When you have a plan of attack for how you are going to earn your advanced degree, start your business, write your book, prepare for retirement, or any other big goal, you put YOWE on the defensive. You are taking charge of the battlefield, choosing where the fight will occur (for example, in the library rather than the saloon), and how it will be fought (for example by investing in mutual funds rather than lottery tickets).

One more thing: Knowing how you're going to achieve your goals does not necessarily mean that you are clear about every step along the way, or that you won't have to make detours as you go along. It means

A great plan of attack will put YOWE on the defensive

that you are able to identify new paths when necessary and that you don't just wander around hoping to somehow stumble upon success and happiness. Having a plan is a roadmap, but it is not the road itself. You will run into obstacles and detours, and occasionally find shortcuts that will get you to your destination more quickly. In his tract on the art of war, von Moltke the elder said that no plan survives contact with the enemy. Or in the more colorful phrasing of boxer Mike Tyson, "Everyone has a plan till they get punched in the mouth."

Don't Settle for Anemic Dreams and Goals

At the end of World War II, both Germany and Japan (and much of the rest of Europe and Asia) lay in ruins. Millions of people faced starvation, and the threat of resurgent violence (such as that which followed the First World War) was all-too-real. In *The Most Noble Adventure: The Marshall Plan and the Time When America Helped Save Europe*, Greg Behrman describes how the gigantic dreams of people like George C. Marshall and Will Clayton to rescue Europe from economic disaster not only saved countless lives and eliminated the danger of yet another worldwide conflagration of violence, it ultimately laid the foundations for the economic unification of Europe and the West's victory in the Cold War. Consider these paradoxes of big goals, then think about how you can make sure that you don't cheat yourself by settling for anemic dreams and goals yourself:

» Big goals are often more likely to be achieved than timid little goals, because they inspire people to extraordinary effort. One of the keys to the success of Apple is that, from the very beginning, Steve Jobs was not just trying to sell computers; he was trying to change the way people learn and work (and more recently, the way they entertain themselves and communicate with one another). He is gone now, but that commitment to thinking big has been woven into Apple's DNA.

» Big goals inspire a higher level of commitment. When Millard Fuller founded Habitat for Humanity his goal was to eradicate poverty housing everywhere in the world. Substantially with volunteer labor and donated supplies the organization has built more than half a million homes worldwide. Had Fuller started with a more timid goal eradicating poverty housing in his home state of Georgia and then growing from there, they would still be stuck in Georgia building their first several houses.

» Big goals often require a proportionately lower level of risk and effort than small goals; you can only take out one second mortgage on a home, and no one can work more than 24 hours a day.

» Once fulfilled, big goals become the platform for even bigger goals. No one could have predicted the technological revolution that would be launched by JFK's big goal of putting a man on the moon, or the worldwide business empire that would spring from Walt Disney's big dream of a new sort of theme park in Anaheim.

If you don't hear YOWE howling at the audacity of your dreams and assuring you that they are a formula for disaster, then you simply are not thinking big enough.

DON'T CHASE WHAT YOU DON'T REALLY WANT

Pierre Boulle's novel *The Bridge Over the River Kwai* (later made into a movie) is set in Burma during the Second World War. In the story, Colonel Nicholson of the British army makes a deal with the commandant of the Japanese prisoner of war camp where he and his men are interned. If the Japanese will let him maintain command of his troops and agree to treat them better, then he will design and build the bridge they need to span the River Kwai so their forces can cross for a planned invasion of India. Unfortunately, Nicholson becomes so obsessed with building the perfect bridge that when British commandos try to blow up that bridge (*his* bridge!) he alerts the Japanese prison guards, warning them to stop the sabotage. He forgot the real objective was to win the war, not to build the bridge. And that cost him his life.

This is a great metaphor for the person who loses sight of what really matters in the pursuit of an ever-expanding list of material desires. Knowing what you really want is often easier said than done, especially with an advertising-driven media creating consumerist appeals that cloud our thinking about what really matters in our lives.

Many people end up so involved in chasing something they say is not really all that important to them – money and the things money will buy (building a bridge) – that they never have time to do the things that give a deeper sense of meaning and purpose to their lives (winning the war). Building the bridge is having a new big screen television set in the family room; winning the war is spending quality time with the family.

YOWE doesn't care about winning the war, only about building the bridge. YOWE is perfectly willing to trade long-term happiness for short-term fun and comfort. No one on their deathbed ever says "I wish I'd watched more TV" or "I wish I'd pumped more quarters into casino slot machines." When I teach classes on values-based life and leadership skills, I'll ask what people most regret in their final days. The same four things come up every time, without exception, and always in the same order:

» Not having spent more time with family and friends (relationships).

» Not having written a book or started a business or traveled the world (experiences).

» Not having done a better job of planning and saving for retirement (finances)

» Not having exercised more, eaten better, and taken better care of the body (health).

No one on their deathbed ever said "I wish I'd watch more TV"

How can you transform your bridge-building activities into war-winning goals? What can you start doing now to assure that you don't experience those regrets in your own final days? What can you do now to start treating the person you will be in the future like a dear friend for whom you have a great responsibility and not like a total stranger for whom you have no obligation?

DON'T WANT WHAT YOU CAN'T HAVE

On April 2 of 1982 Argentina invaded and occupied the Falkland Islands (which they call Islas Malvinas). These islands had been part of the British Empire since 1841 and most of the inhabitants were of British descent. The military junta that ruled Argentina was betting that the British would not risk going to war over the islands. The Generalissimos were wrong. By the middle of June, Argentine forces had been defeated and dislodged from the islands at a cost of more than 2,000 casualties and serious damage to their naval and air fleets. The junta lost credibility at home and was quickly thrown out of office. Argentina still lays claim to the Falkland Islands, but as long as Great Britain has the stronger military force the Argentinians will keep wanting what they can never have.

Influencing you to want what you cannot legitimately have is one of YOWE's most destructive weapons. It is the cause of embezzlement, extramarital affairs, plagiarism, misrepresentation and all sorts of other misdeeds. It is the driving force behind envy, jealousy, greed, and other emotional vices. When you make the leap from wanting what you can't have to trying to get it anyway, you are setting yourself up for a fall because the only way you could possibly succeed in getting that which is otherwise unattainable is to cheat – cheat on your spouse, cheat your customers, cheat your employer, cheat on your taxes, cheat on the test, and eventually cheat yourself.

The tabloids are packed with stories of cheaters taking a fall – CEOs being hauled to jail in handcuffs, disgraced husbands being raked through the judicial system by spouses determined to exact huge alimony settlements, politicians being voted out of office because they violated the trust of the electorate, athletes being stripped of medals because they used illegal performance-enhancing drugs, academics being stripped of their titles because they cheated on their research.

Cheaters almost invariably end up being caught. When that happens, the only winner is YOWE, because being exposed and humiliated gives it one more way to put you in the role of victim. YOWE loves it when you're a victim.

Trying to get what you cannot legitimately have will set you up for a fall

APPRECIATE YOUR BLESSINGS

"Good God, did we really send men to fight in that {blasted wasteland of knee-deep mud and flooded trenches}?"

General Douglas Haig's Chief of Staff upon being taken toward the frontline at Ypres during the First World War (as he burst into tears).

"It gets worse further on up."

His companion who'd already been to the front line trenches

It does not take a very deep study of history – and especially the history of warfare – to appreciate how affluent, comfortable, convenient, and secure life is in the contemporary western world.

Unfortunately, neither does it take much time sitting in an airport before you start hearing people complaining about what have come to be known as "first world problems." If you can decide what to have for dinner because it's what you're in the mood for and not because what's on the plate in front of you is the only thing standing between you and starvation, most of your complaining is probably about first world problems.

The irony of the contrast between the reality of our affluent and comfortable existence and the magnitude of whining and complaining was brilliantly captured by comedian Louis C.K. when comments he made on a late night TV show were posted on YouTube with the title "Everything's Amazing and Nobody's Happy" (which as of this writing has been viewed more than 4 million times). Everybody on every airplane, he says, should constantly be grabbing the arm rests and hollering "Oh my God – WOW!" What greater privilege than to be "sitting in a chair in the sky" looking down on the world below?

I've been in airplanes flying over the Grand Canyon, the Rocky Mountains, and Alaska glaciers where nobody else is even looking out the window. Unless there happens to be a three-year-old onboard, you're not likely to hear anyone shouting "Oh Wow!" – and before the plane lands you're certain to hear people whine about the experience.

Leonardo Da Vinci was probably the most creative man who ever lived. He spent his life fantasizing about flying. His notebooks are filled with sketches and drawings of flying machines. He would have given anything for a window seat on a regional jet flying from Denver to Kalispell and being able to look down upon the clouds and the mountains. And one guesses that over and over he would have been saying, "Oh, Wow! Oh Wow!" (which, by the way, also happened to have been the last words of Steve Jobs, another of history's great cre-

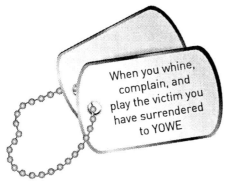

When you whine, complain, and play the victim you have surrendered to YOWE

ative geniuses, as recounted in the biography by Walter Isaacson).

It's a safe bet that there's a whole lot more that's right with your life than there is wrong with it. Any time you catch yourself complaining, or playing the martyr or the victim, you are allowing YOWE to focus your atten-

tion on what's wrong and on the past instead of on what's right and the future. So instead of whining about it, put a smile on your face and shout "Oh my God! WOW!!!" Then say thank you and get back to work.

GET THE PICKLE OUT OF YOUR MOUTH

My father once told me that the two most memorable flights he'd ever taken were the one that took him to Vietnam in 1968 and the one that brought him home in 1969.

Several years ago I boarded an airplane and sat across the aisle from a taut pile of muscles crammed into a too-tight Gold's Gym tank top. The guy looked like he could bend a railroad spike with his bare hands and then eat it for breakfast. He looked like Superman on steroids. At least until he opened his mouth. After he'd sat down, he pulled out his cell phone and launched into the most pitiable whine-fest. You would have thought the entire airline industry had engaged in a conspiracy to ruin his life because his flight arrived late and he hadn't had a chance to stop at Starbucks because he'd booked too tight a connection. Poor crybaby – I wanted to hand him a pacifier.

I'm old enough to remember when airport food was a bologna sandwich in a baggie; airplane cockpits filled with toxic cigarette smoke the minute the seatbelt light went out; "lost bag" meant en route to Asia; and "missed flight" meant spending a night or two on the floor of the airport. Today airport food is Chili's, Wolfgang Puck, or gourmet popcorn; anyone lighting a cigarette on an airplane would be escorted to the door, parachute or not; "lost bag" means they'll deliver it to your home or hotel, usually before the end of the day; and "missed flight" (often because you tried to book them too close together) means waiting a few hours for the next one, or spending the night in a hotel room at the airline's expense.

I am amazed that – despite all the challenges of the economy, fuel prices, weather, and everything else that complicates their jobs – the airlines get everyone (and I mean millions of us, every day of the week) where we want to go in one piece, almost always on the day we want to be there (usually within minutes of the advertised arrival time), and almost always with our bags in tow. And still people moan and whine at the slightest nuisance, as though the world owes it to them to move every inconvenience out of their way.

Anytime you complain – about anything – what you are really saying is "Poor me – I'm a victim."

Complaining about delayed or canceled flights, or about uncomfortable seats on a regional jet? Poor baby – you are being victimized by the airline that's about to take you from Detroit to Orlando in less than two hours.

Complaining about how much of your income goes to taxes? Poor baby – you are being victimized by the IRS because you happen to make more money than 98% of the rest of the world's population.

Complaining about how overworked, underpaid, and unappreciated you are at work? Poor baby – you are being victimized by a heartless employer who has you trapped in a job that would be considered a cushy and lucrative sinecure almost everywhere else in the world.

I recently watched a TED Talk by a woman who had been severely burned when someone ran head-on into her car and it caught fire. She spent more than a year in the hospital in almost constant debilitating pain. Today she travels the world speaking about courage and compassion, and has started a nonprofit foundation to take severely burned and disfigured kids on outdoor adventures. She refused to allow personal tragedy to make her a victim.

When bad things happen to good people (when, not if) those people have a choice to make. Bad things that have happened almost never unhappen. So you can play the role of the victim and keep complaining. Or you can work to make something positive come from the experience. Nothing bad can a happen to you that does not have the potential to be the catalyst for something good. That is the premise that underlies The Pickle Pledge. We call it that because chronic complainers look, at least metaphorically, like they've been sucking on a dill pickle. Please take a minute to read this promise, including the footnote.

Keeping this promise can change your life. I know it has changed mine. After Lasik eye surgery performed by a dishonest and incompetent surgeon left me with severe double vision, impaired visual acuity, and chronic eye pain, I had a choice to make: I could keep whining and being the victim, or I could do something about it.

I have since done the research, written a report on things someone should know before getting Lasik, and have posted a number of videos that collectively have more than 100,000 views. I've counseled other Lasik casualties (including at least two young people who were contemplating suicide because of the damage done to their eyes by Lasik), and have heard from a number of others who decided that the risks of this elective cosmetic surgery on the only pair of eyes they will ever be blessed with were too great, and that they were happy with glasses or contacts after all.

And you know what? – I prefer the angry activist I am now over the pathetic victim I'd been playing before I took The Pickle Pledge to heart.

One more thing. Because toxic emotional negativity is the emotional and spiritual equivalent of cigarette smoke, and in its way just as malignant, take the next step by declaring your workplace, and your home, to be a Pickle Free Zone.

Pickle-Free Zone door hangers are available at
www.ValuesCoach.com/store

REFRAME YOUR PAST

Every historian knows that "the past" is what you choose to remember, and how you choose to remember it. A Union artillery officer and a Confederate foot soldier might both have been at Gettysburg on the day of Pickett's Charge, but they will have very different memories of what happened that day, and would write very different narratives of the causes of the war and the righteousness of the combatants.

It's the same with you. Your best self and YOWE will remember the things that have happened in your past in very different ways. YOWE will always interpret past occurrences in a way that places you in the victim role, one way or another. YOWE loves it when you can wallow around in self-pity and blame others for your low self-esteem and poor self-image, and for the fact that you are not living up to your true potential.

During my teen years I was often in trouble. To this day, whenever I see a chalkboard the words "I will not…" pop into my head because back then I'd written so many sentences beginning with those words. One day a teacher, apparently at his wit's  end because nothing else had worked, placed a folding chair in an empty section of the trophy case in the main corridor and made me sit in it, with a list of my "crimes" posted on the glass. I felt like a monkey in the zoo looking through the bars of his cage while the girls pointed and giggled as they passed by. Now, as you might imagine, this did not boost my self-esteem. For years, that memory was an integral part of my self-image: troublemaker, outsider, the one who got attention by breaking rules rather than by doing good work.

The past is what you choose to remember – make it a good one

Then one day it occurred to me to ask what that teacher's motives might have been. Had he really taken a sadistic joy in my humiliation? Or did he suspect that unless I changed my ways someday I would end up in much bigger trouble? Was he trying to warn me that, one way or another, people who sought attention by breaking the rules usually end up in a cage of some sort? And if it was the latter, why was I allowing YOWE to use that memory as an excuse for sitting in my own invisible cage of self-imposed limitations?

Think of your own most painful memories. How can you change your perspective, reframe those memories, and let go of the deadweight of the past that, if you persist in hanging on to it, will diminish your future?

STRENGTHEN THE POWER OF BELIEF

When Admiral DuPont reported to Admiral Farragut the failure of Union ships under his command to break into Confederate-held Charleston Harbor during the Civil War, he recounted all the excuses for his defeat. After he'd finished Farragut replied, "DuPont, there was one reason more. You did not break into that harbor because you did not believe you could do it." The following year, Farragut himself demonstrated the power of belief. He had himself tied to the mast of his flagship as he led the Union fleet into Mobile Harbor. When one of his ships was sunk by a Confederate mine Farragut hollered, "Damn the torpedoes, full speed ahead." By the end of the day, Mobile was his.

The Bible tells us that all things are possible for one who believes (Mark 9:23). In the classic self-help book *Think and Grow Rich* Napoleon Hill wrote, "What the mind can conceive *and believe* it can achieve" (emphasis added). Belief is the force behind hope and optimism. But here's the deal: belief does not spontaneously materialize in the mind – it is the result of concentrated

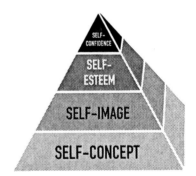

THE PYRAMID OF SELF-BELIEF

mental effort and seeing the results of your work come to fruition. You earn belief in your dreams and goals first by keeping a clear mental image of the dream fulfilled and the goal achieved front and center in your consciousness, and second by making a commitment to sustained action toward those dreams and goals.

Self-belief is developed at four levels. Imagine a 4-step pyramid, with self-concept at the foundation and self-confidence at the top. Each element builds upon those below:

» **Level One, Self-Concept:** An underlying awareness, either implicit or explicit, of your role as a human being in this universe. What do you see when you look around you: a world of scarcity and risk, or a world of abundance and opportunity? Evidence for both views abounds, though we tend to see what we look for. What is your concept of a higher power, and of your relationship to that higher power? Someone who believes in a God of judgmental wrath will lead a very different life than the person who believes in a God of love and mercy, or someone who places God in the same mental box as Santa Claus and the Easter Bunny. Questions like these cannot be answered in an absolute sense, but rather depend largely on what you choose to see as you look around you and within you. Your self-concept will have a profound influence on your personality and upon the results you get in life.

» **Level Two, Self-Image:** What do you see when you look in the mirror? A winner? A victim? A loser? You will never on a sustained basis exceed your self-image. If your self-image is

that of victim, no matter what happens you will always be a victim. One of the main reasons that a majority of those who "win" big in the lottery end up bankrupt within a year or so is that they still see a victim when they look in the mirror, and end up blowing all their money to establish consistency between that inner self image of victim and the outer reality of winner. On the other hand, the self-perceived winner who loses everything

You will never exceed your self-image

will eventually find a way to get it all back. She simply won't be able to live in a world where her outer reality is inconsistent with her inner reality.

» **Level Three, Self-Esteem:** Do you like what you see when you look in the mirror? Do you believe you are capable of achieving your dreams and goals, and that you deserve to enjoy the fruits of your success? Do you believe you are worthy of the affection and respect of other people? People with high self-esteem get a lot done and make substantial contributions; people with low self-esteem tend not to. Low self-esteem is often an insidious excuse for cowardice (fear of rejection) and laziness (fear of failure). Real self-esteem is the product of hard work.

» **Level Four, Self-Confidence:** This means that you feel like you have what it takes in terms of skills and resources to meet the challenges of your life and to effectively pursue your dreams and goals, or you are reasonably certain that you can obtain whatever you need but are now lacking. Genuine self-confidence is usually quiet, as opposed to the loud boastfulness of arrogance.

To enhance self-belief it is often best to start at the top of the pyramid by working on self-confidence. An example: if your finances are out of control and you're over your head in debt, you most likely lack confidence in your money management skills. Your self-esteem suffers with every call from a creditor demanding payment on an overdue bill. Your self-image is that of a victim and not of a winner. And you can't see the opportunities and abundance in the world around you because your vision is fixated on the scarcity right in front of you.

So you go to the bookstore, buy *The Total Money Makeover*, and do what Dave Ramsey tells you to do. You spend less, save more, and make better investment decisions. As you get your finances under control and stop getting threatening calls from bill collectors your confidence goes up – you discover that you really can manage your money. That enhances your self-esteem, and your self-image gradually transforms from victim to winner. And as your financial picture improves your self-concept broadens as you see opportunities for investing and contributing that you were blind to before.

Warning: The more successful you are at keeping money in the bank, the more powerful will be your urges to celebrate with a shopping spree or a Caribbean cruise. But now you know what those urges are – sneak attacks by YOWE. Don't give in to them.

GET THE WORDS RIGHT

Every war, including the war with YOWE, is a war of words. The words we use to describe the world around us, and the world within us, substantially determine our attitudes, beliefs, and actions. In the darkest days of World War II, Winston Churchill galvanized a nation with his oratory ("We shall never surrender!"). Josef Stalin repositioned the greatest military catastrophe in the history of the world – the devastating losses the Soviet armies suffered in the first months of the German invasion – into "the great patriotic war" that inspired Russians to endure unimaginable hardships en route to total victory. His Order #227 commanding the battered Soviet Army to stand its ground with the words "not one step back" was brutal in the extreme, but those words inspired the tenacity behind the defense of Stalingrad, which was one of the crucial turning points of that war.

Whenever you speak, and whatever you say, you are first and foremost speaking to yourself. YOWE is always listening, and usually talking back like a truculent (and occasionally obscene) teenager. When you tell someone that you will "try" to finish a project or meet a deadline, YOWE interprets that as permission to knock off for the day and leave the trying for tomorrow. Of course, when the deadline is missed YOWE will reassure you with the consolation that at least you tried. When Yoda told Luke Skywalker "Do or do not, there is no try," he was telling the young man (and those of us watching the scene on the silver screen) to give YOWE a swift kick in the rear and make a commitment to achieve a result instead of offering to try.

Words have power. Words shape reality as perceived by you (and by YOWE). Use them in ways that give you power and never in ways that give that power away. So, for example, when someone asks you how you're doing, never reply "I'm hanging in there." Who hangs? Criminals hang. Desperate people hang. Monkeys hang. Whenever you tell someone that you're "hanging in there," whether you realize it or not, what you are really telling them – and yourself – is that things aren't going well.

When someone asks how you're doing, tell them that you're doing great. Even if you don't feel like it, say the words. Getting the words right is often the first step toward changing the reality.

Getting the words right is the first step towards changing your reality

Part 3 of this book includes the seven simple (but by no means always easy) promises of The Self Empowerment Pledge: Responsibility, Accountability, Determination, Contribution, Resilience, Perspective, and Faith. Commit yourself to memorizing and internalizing the words from these seven promises. It will be one of the best investments you ever make in yourself.

Start now with the free PledgePower app which allows you to program daily reminders, message other people, read the motivational message of the day, and more.

THE SELF EMPOWERMENT
PLEDGE
Seven Simple Promises That Will Change Your Life

Monday's Promise:
Responsibility
I will take complete responsibility for my health, my happiness, my success, and my life, and will not blame others for my problems or predicaments.

Tuesday's Promise:
Accountability
I will not allow low self-esteem, self-limiting beliefs, or the negativity of others to prevent me from achieving my authentic goals and from becoming the person I am meant to be.

Wednesday's Promise:
Determination
I will do the things I'm afraid to do, but which I know should be done. Sometimes this will mean asking for help to do that which I cannot do by myself.

Thursday's Promise:
Contribution
I will earn the help I need in advance by helping other people now, and repay the help I receive by serving others later.

Friday's Promise:
Resilience
I will face rejection and failure with courage, awareness, and perseverance, making these experiences the platform for future acceptance and success.

Saturday's Promise:
Perspective
Though I might not understand why adversity happens, by my conscious choice I will find strength, compassion, and grace through my trials.

Sunday's Promise: Faith
My faith and my gratitude for that I have been blessed with will shine through in my attitudes and in my actions.

www.Pledge-Power.com

RAISE YOUR SELF-ESTEEM

Did you see the movie *Patton* with George C. Scott playing the role of the great general? It contains a great lesson in how to raise self-esteem – your own and that of those who depend upon you – by raising your standards and expectations.

When Patton first took command of II Corps in Tunisia the troops were slovenly and disheveled. They had been clobbered by Rommel in the battle of Kasserine Pass; morale was low and discipline lax. Their appearance was, in Patton's view, a reflection of poor self-esteem that would, he believed, get many of them killed in battle if allowed to persist. Knowing they would soon be back in action, Patton imposed stiff fines on soldiers (and nurses!) caught out of uniform, not wearing helmets, or otherwise not comporting themselves with proper martial discipline. In short order, II Corps was transformed into an effective fighting force and soon was besting Rommel's famed Afrika Corps on the battlefield.

Low self-esteem is almost always a reflection of YOWE at work. It is often an insidious excuse for laziness (if you think you're bound to fail, it's easy to find reasons to not even try) and for cowardice (if you assume that you're going to be rejected, you'll find excuses to not ask in the first place). People with low self-esteem almost always end up being their own worst enemies, one way or another. For example, they tend to have ambivalent feelings about money; they want it, but subconsciously feel they  don't deserve very much of it. Therefore, when they come into money, rather than being responsible stewards they tend to blow it on things they don't really need (or even really want). Here's my formula for winning the war with yourself on the self-esteem front:

1. Accept yourself as you are, warts and all. Don't pretend to be someone you're not because you think you'll impress people or make more money by being a fake than you would by being genuine. Figure out your few great strengths and passions and cultivate them.

2. Work on the warts. I don't mean to try and fix all of your weaknesses (we each have far too many weaknesses to correct them all, and it takes time away from developing our strengths). I mean the warts – the character flaws that cause you to act in ways that reflect your lesser self (and we all have these warts).

3. Accept absolute responsibility for your circumstances and your outcomes. You are where you are today because of choices you have made in the past, and no other reason. You will be where you are in the future as a result of choices you make beginning today, and no other reason.

4. Program yourself with positive self-talk. YOWE will talk to you in abusive ways that you would never tolerate from anyone else. Reclaim your inner podium by re-scripting that inner dialog to be more positive and more affirming.

5. Decide to have energy. It takes more energy to be happy than it does to be miserable, and yes, whether or not you have energy is more often than not a decision and not a physiological state. When you walk in the front door after a hard day at work and head for the TV instead of the exercise

machine, you have *decided* to be lethargic. You are waving the white flag of surrender to YOWE.

6. Be more disciplined in planning and using time. People with low self-esteem are notoriously poor time managers. One of the most immediate ways you can begin raising your self-esteem is by putting your time to more effective use. Napoleon said he would yield space, but never lose time.

7. At all costs avoid negative people, and go out of your way to seek out positive people. Over time, you take on the attitudes of the people you hang around with. Stay away from the cynics, the critics, the emotional vampires, and the people who make themselves feel big by trying to make you feel small.

8. Finally, believe in other people. It's hard for you to believe in yourself if you don't believe in others, and others will find it hard to believe in you if they sense that you don't believe in them. Be a Dionarap (don't try to look that word up because I made it up). Dionarap is the word paranoid spelled backwards. If you assume that other people like you and want to help you be successful, that will more often be the case than if you think people don't like you and are out to get you.

FACE REALITY

"Nothing so steadies a company confronting great odds as a sober recitation of the facts. The more dread-inducing the reality, the more directly it must be faced."

Steven Pressfield: *The Virtues of War: A Novel of Alexander the Great*

Nearly 2,500 years ago, Sun Tzu wrote in *The Art of War* that if you know yourself and you know your enemy, you will never be defeated even in one hundred battles, and that if you know the terrain and you know the weather, you will become invincible. Hitler thought he could hold continental Europe, bomb Britain into submission, take Moscow, secure the Balkans and Norway, and declare war on the United States all at once. That master of self-delusion moved imaginary divisions around on the map in his command bunker as the soldiers of his Sixth Army, surrounded and outnumbered at Stalingrad, died by the thousands. Hitler's was an extreme case of delusional thinking, but serves as a warning to anyone whose personal theme song is some variation of "Oh Lord won't you buy me a Mercedes Benz" (with apologies to the late Janis Joplin).

In *The Road Less Traveled* Scott Peck defined mental health as a commitment to face reality, no matter how painful and no matter what the cost. You defeat YOWE when you accept the facts as they really are, not as they used to be, as you think they should be, as you wish they were, or as you fear they might become. As science fiction novelist Philip K. Dick put it: "Reality is that which, when you stop believing in it, doesn't go away." Just because you believe something (or want to believe it) doesn't make it true. And just because you don't believe something (or don't want to believe it) doesn't make it false.

Imagine that the most hard-nosed, tough-minded auditor who ever peeked into the dark corners of an organization spent a week examining every dimension of your life. What trouble spots might that auditor find that you have been trying to ignore in your finances? In your career? In your relationships with others?

Hitler's mortal foe Winston Churchill told the British people that he could offer only blood, sweat, toil and tears. When his army was surrounded at Dunkirk he didn't fantasize about miraculous relief operations of the sort with which Hitler doomed his Sixth Army at Stalingrad. He looked reality square in the face, acknowledged the hopelessness of the situation, and mobilized every seaworthy craft on the English Channel in the rescue operation that we today remember as the Miracle of Dunkirk.

The truth shall set you free. It's ancient wisdom, but to free yourself from the stranglehold of YOWE and its fantasies you must face your truths. And the uglier that truth is, the more urgently you must come to grips with it. The truth will indeed set you free – but first it's likely to really piss you off. Facing that truth is the essential first step in making the transition from wishful thinking to positive thinking. Here's the difference: Wishful thinking is hoping for

Just because you believe something doesn't make it true

something and waiting for someone else to make it happen; positive thinking is *expecting* something and then *working* to make it happen.

BE OBJECTIVE

Underpinning the tragedy of the Vietnam War (which in Vietnam is remembered as the American War) was a persistent refusal by political and military leaders, first in France and then in the United States, to objectively assess the social, geographic, and military realities on the ground. In 1969 Henry Kissinger instructed National Security Council staff to prepare a plan for inflicting catastrophic damage upon North Vietnam, up to and including selected use of nuclear weapons. "I refuse to believe that a little fourth-rate power like North Vietnam does not have a breaking point," he insisted. Four years and many thousands of deaths later, it was the U.S. that reached a breaking point.

In *The Art of War* Sun Tzu warned against underestimating or overestimating the strength of an enemy. In the early days of personal computing, IBM seriously underestimated the strength of Bill Gates and "the kids" at Microsoft, and lost leadership in a vital industry segment as a result. On the other hand, Steve Jobs never overestimated the power of much larger competitors as Apple revolutionized one industry after another.

It's often said that the stock market is driven by two forces: greed in bull markets and fear in bear markets. Using that as a metaphor, YOWE uses greed to cause you to underestimate the nature of a challenge and overestimate the capacity of your resources, and take on unacceptably high levels of risk in the hopes of a quick score. That's why people buy Powerball tickets when the odds of winning are less than 1-in-175 million; that's why they throw away dollars and burn up hours sitting in front of slot machines hoping against hope for an inanimate object to ring the bell that will change their lives.

And YOWE uses fear to cause you to overestimate the nature of the challenge and underestimate the capacity of your own resources and thus become excessively risk-averse and fail to pursue genuine opportunities.

That's why people hang onto a job that offers the illusion of security and don't strike out on their own as freelancers or business owners which, whatever the risks, would give them much greater control over their work, their time, and their lives.

One of the hardest challenges you will face in the war against YOWE is to be objective: to see things as they really are. Not as you think they should be, not as they once were, not as you wish they were, and not as you fear they might become. As they really are.

See things as they really are – not as YOWE portrays them to be

DON'T CONVINCE YOURSELF OF THINGS THAT ARE SIMPLY NOT TRUE

General George B. McClellan has gone down in history as the Civil War General who time after time failed to take action because he had convinced himself that the opposing Confederate forces were larger than they really were – sometimes by a factor of two or three. The consequent lethargy and paralysis on his part caused Abraham Lincoln to famously remark: "If General McClellan does not want to use the army, I would like to borrow it for a time."

One of YOWE's most insidious tricks is the way that it convinces you of things that simply are not true.

Psychologists have shown that people will seek out facts to justify their opinions, rather than form their opinions based upon the facts. The Bush-Cheney administration had convinced itself that the U.S.

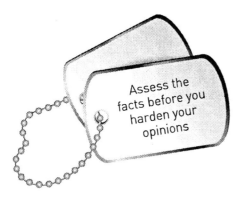

was endangered by imagined weapons of mass destruction in Iraq and sought out "facts" with which to document that opinion, with tragic consequences for both nations and the entire Mideast region.

Convincing yourself of things that simply are not true is one of YOWE's most effective weapons for keeping you in a state of anxiety and depression. At the first suspicion that you are being cheated, or cheated on, YOWE will manufacture vivid mental images of the dastardly act. Unless you recognize what YOWE is doing and stop it you run the risk of paranoia poisoning relationships because in your mind you see people doing things that they have never actually done in the physical world.

At the extreme, convincing yourself of things that simply are not true can result in poverty and even death. Every year or so, as one example, we read about some charismatic minister who has convinced his flock that the world will end on a certain day. They sell all of their possessions. On the presumed day of reckoning they gather to pray and hold their breath as the end – does not come. The sun rises again as it has every day for billions of years, and as it will continue doing for billions more years, leaving them impoverished and potentially suicidal.

The Four Way Test of Rotary International asks: Is it the truth? That's a good question for you to ask any time you catch yourself ruminating on bad things you imagine happening or bad things you imagine other people doing.

CHANGE YOUR REFERENCE GROUP

"The world is a powerful conditioner. It's working on you all the time – negativity is normal, positivity is abnormal. To win, you must train to beat that external conditioning, to overcome the brainwashing exerted by a powerful world of negative influence. You must follow a separate path."

James Loehr and Peter McLaughlin: *Mentally Tough:*
The Principles of Winning at Sports Applied to Winning in Business

During my undergraduate years I wrote a thesis on the social and economic impact of the German hyperinflation of the post-World War I era, which I concluded played a more important role in setting the stage for Hitler and World War II than did the Great Depression of the following decade. One of the most surprising findings was that it was easier for right wing radicals in the Nazi and Nationalist parties to recruit from the ranks of left wing radicals in the Communist and Spartacist organizations, and vice versa, than it was for either to recruit from the middle class. During these violent and chaotic years, people were profoundly influenced by the opinions and attitudes of the people around them. Tragically, as the Nazi Party emerged as the dominant force in German politics, peer pressure from a rapidly expanding reference group was at least initially more important than Gestapo terror in bringing the mass of Germans into line.

Sociologists tell us that one of the most important, if not *the* most important, influences on our lives is the people we spend time with, the people with whom we identify. This is what they call our reference group. People tend to hang around with others who are like them in terms of race, attitudes, political opinions, religious beliefs, and income level. We are all profoundly imprinted by the characteristics of the reference groups with which we identify, in both conscious and subconscious ways.

If your reference group consists primarily of people who are depressed, pessimistic, and chronically whining about how the world has made them a victim, over time it will be almost impossible for you to not fall into that emotional quicksand. On the other hand, if you are depressed and anxious but start to spend time with people who are confident and optimistic, their attitudes will rub off on you. One of the surest ways to enhance your courage is to change your reference groups. You do this by consciously seeking out people who have the qualities you would like to emulate.  This entails sticking your neck out, networking more, joining Rotary or the Optimist Club, and otherwise getting out of your shell.

Just as a recovering alcoholic can no longer go into a bar, or a recovering smoker needs to stop hanging around with other smokers, as soon as the complaining, whining, and gossiping starts, you need to close your ears, and if possible get up and leave the room.

A cancer survivor once told me that one of the most important things she did for her recovery was refuse to participate in toxic emotional negativity. She said that she was amazed at how toxic emotional negativity drained her of the energy she needed to fight the cancer, and how much brighter her life became when she refused to be a part of it. She said: "I learned the difference between a true friend and a bitch buddy, and decided I wanted more of the former and none of the latter."

To beat YOWE, you need to follow her example. Stop wasting your time (and your life) hanging around with negative, cynical, pessimistic bitch buddies and instead keep the company of positive people who are determined to get things done.

YOU NEED FRIENDLY CRITICS

Winston Churchill said that the only thing worse than fighting with allies was fighting without them. The best allies are those who will tell you hard truths – the ones you don't want to hear, but need to hear. As I write this, I've just returned from a meeting of the Values Coach Advisory Board. Its members are all close friends – people I love and admire. Here are some of the questions they asked during the meeting:

» Do you feel like you don't deserve to be surrounded by a great team?

» You are holding a winning lottery ticket – what's it going to take to get you to go cash it in?

» Do you really want to change the world or are you content to have a comfortable lifestyle business as a speaker and author?

» Why aren't you converting more of your one-off leadership retreats into longer-term client relationships?

» Why aren't you famous yet? You've got a much more powerful message – and present it far more effectively – than a lot of people who are famous. Is this a self-esteem problem?

It was, I don't need to tell you, a very humbling experience. It took courage for my friends to say what they said – and I hope that I had the wisdom to really listen. Good friends are willing to tell a naked emperor that he has no clothes on, and a wise emperor will listen to what they tell him.

My friend David Corbin – author of the book *Illuminate: Harnessing the Positive Power of Negative Thinking* – says that he makes his living as a consultant but he earns his keep as an insultant, telling people things they need to hear but don't want to hear.

You need friends who have the courage to tell you that no one else can see the kingly clothes you are so proud to be wearing. And you need to listen to them when they do.

Stay away from pickle suckers, emotional vampires, and bitch buddies

TRAIN YOUR DOUBT

"No important undertaking was ever yet carried out without the Commander having to subdue new doubts in himself at the time of commencing the execution of his work."

Carl von Clausewitz: *On War*

In Shakespeare's play *Measure for Measure,* Lucio counsels Isabella saying: "Our doubts are traitors, and make us lose the good we might win by fearing to attempt." Doubt is one of the weapons YOWE uses to prevent you from making decisions and from taking action. Just when you think a decision has been reached and you are ready to make a commitment, new information comes in, new questions arise, and new doubts cause you to pause, reconsider, postpone, and eventually the dream dies – strangled in this web of doubt.

That's how YOWE works. First it sends along doubt to soften you up. You begin to doubt whether or not you're doing things right. Then you doubt whether you're doing the right thing. And finally you doubt whether you're even the right person to be doing those things. Once there is enough doubt, once you stop believing in yourself, YOWE knows it can defeat you.

The good news is that you can make doubt work for you. In the ninth of his ten letters to a certain Mr. Kappus (*Letters to a Young Poet,* written in 1903-1904) the German poet Rainer Maria Rilke advised the young would-be poet to train his doubt, to turn it into a positive and constructive form of questioning. Rilke wrote:

Ask [your doubt] – whenever it wants to spoil something for you – *why* something is ugly. Demand proofs from it, test it, and you will find it perhaps bewildered and embarrassed, perhaps also protesting. But don't give in, insist on arguments, and act in this way, attentive and persistent, every single time, and the day will come when instead of being a destroyer, it will become one of your best workers – perhaps the most intelligent of all the ones that are building your life. (emphasis in original)

Note how Rilke described doubt as an entity outside of the true self – something to being argued with – in much the same way that I've described YOWE as something alien to your authentic self. YOWE uses doubt to kill your dreams with imagined rejection, failure, and humiliation. You must counterattack by questioning, arguing with it, "demanding proofs from it" and challenging it to continue the conversation by forcing it to ask better questions of you.

Train your doubt to be an ally by forcing it to ask empowering questions

Doubt becomes your ally when you force it to change "that will never work" to "what else must be done to make sure that it does work?" or "what are the next steps if it doesn't work?" Doubt becomes your ally when it helps you uncover areas of your own ignorance; when it causes you to replace complacence with caution and arrogance with humility; and when it guides you to answers for those better questions you have challenged it to raise.

ACT THE PART

In her biography of Alexander the Great, Mary Renault referred to his "sense of theatre." In *Mask of Command*, John Keegan's study of different styles of military leadership, he describes the manner in which Alexander stopped a mutiny by some of his veteran troops as "one of the supreme performances of political theater... Like a great actor in a great role, being and performance merged in [Alexander's] person." Before speaking to his soldiers George Patton, who believed that in a previous incarnation he had fought beside Alexander, would stand in front of a mirror and practice his "war face." Great commanders know that you cannot inspire the troops with a memo, or by standing at a podium reading a script. They recognize that you must act the part before you can be the part.

As of this writing, Harvard Business School Professor Amy Cuddy's TED Talk "Your Body Language Shapes Who You Are" has been viewed more than 30 million times. She prescribes "power posing" as a way to change your own self-image and the way you are perceived by others – including YOWE. Don't just fake it till you make it, she says – fake it till you become it.

Remember – YOWE is fundamentally a coward and will back down at any show of determined power on your part. So put on your war face, position your body in a power pose, stare down YOWE, and get to work.

ROAR!

Did you see *Return of the King*, the third movie in *The Lord of the Rings* trilogy? Before leading his men (and one remarkable woman) into the climactic battle against the forces of Mordor, King Theoden rode down the line clashing his sword against his warrior's spears. And then with a mighty roar he led his army galloping into combat.

Several years ago a friend called me with a problem. He sold medical devices and had just received a promotion. That's great, I said, so what's the problem?

He told me that his new job entailed going into operating rooms with surgeons, and that he fainted at the sight of blood.

Hmm, I said, that *is* a problem.

I suggested that every morning when he got out of bed he visualize his fear of passing out at the sight of blood as a hideous monster with bloody fangs barring the door of his bedroom. I told him to put on his war face (remember Patton's war face?), clench his fists, take a step toward that monster and ROAR like a ferocious lion. I told him to visualize that hideous monster turning tail and running away. Then to repeat the process at least four more times.

Fear is a cage with no lock on the door

I told him to keep doing this until it became so permanently wired into his mind that he could achieve the same effect without actually ROARing out loud. I pointed out that if he ROARed at the door of the operating room they would not let him in.

My friend rarely goes into operating rooms anymore because he's been promoted again. Now he travels the world supervising other people who go into those operating rooms. But the non-negotiable first step was for him to stare down and chase away the monster of fear, the shadow of YOWE.

Fear is a cage with no lock on the door. And sometimes all it takes is a mighty ROAR to make that door swing open.

GET YOUR Z'S

"Fatigue makes cowards of us all."

Vince Lombardi

In his book *Dreamland: Adventures in the Strange Science of Sleep* David K. Randall writes about how sleep-deprived U.S. soldiers in Iraq and Afghanistan have occasionally behaved in ways that undermined the mission of winning the hearts and minds of the local populace. He says: "Grumpy, tired soldiers have less control over their emotions and are therefore more likely to get into a fight with civilians. Those civilians, in turn, are more likely to have a negative view of American forces and their presence in their country."

Think of it. Our government spends hundreds of billions of dollars to send military forces halfway around the world, resulting in tens of thousands of casualties, with a goal of simultaneously winning two wars. But the entire enterprise becomes jeopardized by the behavior of a handful of sleep-deprived soldiers. It's a metaphor – and a warning – for what can happen when you don't have good sleep habits yourself. In that state you are more prone to anxiety and depression, less likely to project confidence and optimism in your interactions with others, and more likely to shoot yourself in the foot by reacting emotionally when you should be responding rationally.

When you stay up past bedtime watching late night TV, it's YOWE keeping your finger from pressing the off button on the remote. When you're up half the night worrying, it's YOWE creating mental images of doom and disaster. YOWE loves to keep you sleep-deprived because it makes it so much easier to defeat you.

In his book *The Way We're Working Isn't Working* Tony Schwartz writes that chronic sleep deprivation is the number one drag on productivity in America, and the number one cause of individuals not achieving their goals and living up to their full potential.

When YOWE is battering down your defenses, chances are that you've been weakened by inadequate sleep. Whole books have been written on the subject (see for example *Power Sleep* by Peter Maas) and you can find hundreds of references online, but the basics are pretty simple: have a consistent time and routine for bedtime; no caffeine or other stimulants after noon; turn off the TV and the computer at least one hour before going to bed; keep your room as dark and quiet as possible; and leave your worries outside the bedroom where you can be sure they will still be waiting for you in the morning.

And if you can get away with it, practice what I call Neuro Attitudinal Positivity during the day by taking a N.A.P.

THERE'S NO SUCH THING AS FALSE HOPE

"Those who would transform a nation or the world {or themselves}…must know how to kindle and fan an extravagant hope."

Eric Hoffer: *The True Believer*

In the immediate aftermath of the terrorist attacks of 9/11, executives of U.S. air carriers suffered a collective panic attack. Within a few weeks they fired more than 140,000 airline employees, in the process doing serious damage to the global economy – which was precisely what the terrorists had wanted them to do. The then-CEO of United Airlines sent a message to his employees warning that their company could "perish" within less than a year. Can you imagine Winston Churchill having sent such a message to the British people during the darkest days of the Blitz?

The only air carrier that stood strong against the wave of despair that engulfed the airline industry was Southwest Airlines. Southwest's CEO told his people to not worry about losing their jobs. Southwest was a tough company that knew how to handle tough times, he said, and if everyone did their jobs they would be fine.

Substantially as a result of the hopelessness engendered by the managerial cowardice of their leaders, over the succeeding decade every major air carrier, with one exception, went through bankruptcy. The exception was Southwest Airlines.

Narnia author C.S. Lewis said that courage is all of the other virtues at the point where they are tested. The chaotic days following the 9/11 attacks were a moment of truth for the airline industry in which their values were tested. With the exception of Southwest, they all failed that test. At a time when their employees, and their nation, needed hope and courage these highly-paid executives gave in to hopelessness and despair.

Let's make an important distinction here. We are not talking about the hope that is wishful thinking – as in "Gee, I hope everything works out" or "I sure hope I win the lottery." The hope that leaders must inculcate is a much sterner stuff. It is the conviction that whatever happens, we will have the inner strength to not merely make it through but to grow stronger from the experience. It is the hope that Ernest Shackleton gave his men when they were stranded on the Antarctic ice for two years – and without which they all would certainly have died.

I read a book on leadership in which the statement was made that "hope is not a strategy." Other than being a blinding flash of the obvious, it was a remarkably unhelpful and downright misleading comment. To be sure, hope itself is not a strategy, but without hope even the most brilliant of strategies are doomed to fail. The greatest leaders all understand this and they know that their most important job is not just to create and execute brilliant strategies – it is to foster hope on the part of the people whose efforts will be required to implement those strategies.

Franklin D. Roosevelt's team devised brilliant strategies to end the Great Depression, but he knew that these strategies would fail if he was not able to instill the hope that "the only thing we have to fear is fear itself."

Winston Churchill's team devised brilliant strategies to fight the Nazis during World War II, but he knew that his most powerful weapon was using his radio speeches to give his embattled citizens the hope that "we shall never surrender."

Martin Luther King's team devised brilliant strategies to end segregation, but he knew that his biggest challenge was sparking the hope that one day all of us would join him in saying "I have a dream."

I once received a call from a hospital department head asking if Values Coach could help them deal with a toxic level of anxiety within their organization. After hanging up I went to the hospital's website and viewed the video message their CEO had posted. He talked about how changes in the healthcare system would soon make the hospital as we know it obsolete and that we all had to prepare for wrenching change as the hospital disappears from the healthcare landscape.

Then he turned around and walked away, just like that. He said not one word that would give his staff the hope that their hospital would survive, and that they would continue to have jobs in this brave new world of healthcare he had just described. Is it any wonder that the hospital was afflicted with a toxic level of anxiety? This particular CEO had failed the #1 duty of every leader – to instill hope in the face of tough times.

Hope is the platform upon which optimism is built, and optimism is the fuel that powers belief. Whether you're talking about a family, an organization, or an entire community, the leader's most important duty – and the greatest gift that he or she can give – is the power of hope. The beautiful thing about hope is that you don't have to justify it. You can hope that things work out for the best without knowing exactly how that will happen. You can hope for a miracle without knowing exactly what that miracle will be.

MANAGE YOUR ANXIETY

Toxic anxiety is the mortal foe of creative thought, effective decision-making, and decisive action. Norman Dixon's 1976 study *On the Psychology of Military Incompetence* determined that one of the most significant differences between capable and inept commanders was this: the former were able to manage their anxiety and the latter were not. When in the thrall of anxiety, the incompetent commanders were often either paralyzed into inaction or panicked into brash and costly reaction.

Some anxiety can be a good thing. It can prompt you to quit the job that's killing your soul and start the business you've always dreamed of building. It can inspire you to spend more time with a child who seems to be hanging out with the wrong crowd and headed for trouble. It can get you to leave the bar and go to the library to study for the test coming up tomorrow. The anxiety-performance curve demonstrates that some anxiety can improve performance, but that at a certain point more anxiety causes a rapid deterioration.

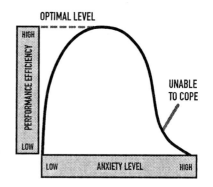

THE PERFORMANCE ANXIETY CURVE

That's because three cognitive distortions can happen when you are in the grip of anxiety:

> » *Distorted memories of the past:* When you're full of anxiety, past failures loom large in your memory and seem almost certain to be repeated while past successes are written off as flukes or dumb luck that would never happen again.

» *Warped perceptions of the present:* In a state of high anxiety, you do not see the world as it really is but rather as you fear it might become. You tend to see strangers as enemies, uncertainty as danger, and molehills as mountains. And you see your strengths as being much less than what they really are.

» *Twisted vision of the future:* Anxiety tends to feed pessimism and poison optimism. The individual who cannot master anxiety has a very hard time imagining a miraculous turn of events, but has no trouble whatsoever in imagining him or herself sleeping under a bridge after having lost everything.

Before we look at why anxiety can be such a serious problem, it's important to understand the difference between anxiety and fear. As philosopher Paul Tillich explained in his book *The Courage to Be*, fear has an object – you are afraid of *something* - whereas anxiety is the vague and formless dread that seems to be an eternal element of the human condition, rooted in the fact that humans are the only species with awareness that their time on earth is finite. It's the over-whelming sense that another shoe is about to drop and not knowing when or from where it will come.

The anxious mind creates enemies were in reality there are none

Anxiety, Tillich said, causes great emotional pain precisely because it is rooted in uncertainty, and we humans need to feel a sense of control. Therefore, the mind strives to transform anxiety into fear, since fear has an object – that something you're afraid of. Being afraid of *something* gives you the illusion of control.

The problem is that the anxious mind creates enemies where in reality there are none. It's the difference between taking a late evening stroll through a safe neighborhood and walking alone at night in a strange city. In the latter, you subconsciously and automatically transform every noise into a stalking mugger. It makes it hard to enjoy the walk, much less to be thinking creatively about new marketing opportunities for your business (unless your business is selling personal security systems or self-defense lessons).

Anxiety, and the state of chronic fear it breeds, can be a prison more confining than iron bars, because you are being imprisoned both physically and mentally. When you are being held under the thumb of your anxiety, you simply cannot see the options that, if successfully pursued, could free you from the anxiety-provoking situation. There are four essential steps to freeing yourself from the Anxiety Trap.

The first is simple awareness - paying attention and keeping your mind in the present. The anxious mind will create all sorts of unpleasant scenarios and then play them repeatedly in the theater of your mind, as if they were certain to occur. Of course, the more your mind fixates on those images of doom and disaster, the more likely it is that they will come to pass. Every time your mind takes off on a Fantasized Experience Appearing Real, you need to gently bring it back into the present.

The second step is to take action. Do the thing you fear, said Ralph Waldo Emerson, and the death of the fear is certain. When you feel yourself in the jaws of the Anxiety Trap, it's important to keep moving. Keep moving physically; sometimes simply going for a jog or a walk can help you pull out of the anxiety trap. Keep moving mentally; if the source of your anxiety is money, get a book or take a course on personal finance. Keep moving emotionally; if you are stuck in a cloud of dread, go see a friend or watch a funny movie. Keep moving spiritually; if you're overwhelmed by unanswered questions about the meaning of life and death, seek out a counselor or read an inspiring book (better yet, do both).

The third step is to be committed to goals that are bigger than you are, and to a mission of vital importance. If you do that, you will soon come to believe that what you are doing is so important, you will simply not be allowed to fail. That will give you a tremendous source of strength in the face of anxiety.

The fourth step is to have faith. The things that cause the greatest anxiety – including our inability to control the world around us and our knowledge that we must one day leave this world – cannot be changed, they can only be accepted. Believe that, whatever happens, you will be supported in ways that cannot be anticipated or explained, and your anxiety will be much more manageable.

One more thing: Faith has its beginning at precisely that point where certainty has its end. The greater the uncertainty, the higher the anxiety, the stronger your faith needs to be.

THE FIGHT IN YOUR DOG

"What matters is not the size of the dog in the fight but rather the size of the fight in the dog."

Dwight D. Eisenhower (quoting Mark Twain)

I have a close friend who is both alcoholic and bulimic, and the two addictions mix together in a toxic sort of cocktail. She drinks to escape from the person she thinks she sees in the mirror: the young girl who was "fat" even though she weighed less than 100 pounds, and who has now "graduated" from anorexia to bulimia. Drinking knocks out any inhibitions she might have about binging and purging, so one addiction leads inevitably to the other. Of course, the next day she feels guilty, which she deals with by having a few drinks and once more raiding the pantry.

My friend showed me a letter from her doctor listing her various medical conditions. It was quite a long list, and included some fairly serious health problems caused by and/or exacerbated by bulimia. At least outwardly she shrugs it off, the way a smoker never believes she will die of lung cancer. My friend's drinking and eating buddy is, of course, YOWE.

Like a great white shark closing in on its prey, or cancer sprouting in a smoker's lungs, YOWE does not care that my friend has family and friends who love her and would be devastated by her loss. In fact that is precisely YOWE's purpose. Freud called it the death drive for a very good reason. YOWE is a predator, YOWE is a parasite – you are the prey and you are the host.

But here's the real heartbreak: for a while my friend was putting up a good fight against YOWE – and she was winning. She was taking Antabuse to control the drinking, reading books on how to beat addiction and gain a greater sense of self-efficacy, and practicing daily affirmations. She was eating healthy. The people around her could see the difference. She was happier, more energized, and more focused on the bright potential of the future than she was on the dead weight of the past.

When the collapse came it was sudden and it was total. She waved the white flag of surrender and YOWE welcomed her back to the bottle and the pantry with open arms – an embrace that will become a noose unless she is somehow able to re-spark the courage and the will to resume the fight.

Remember: fear is a reaction, courage is a decision, and perseverance is making that decision day after day after day. It matters not how many times you fall down, only that you keep getting back up. Every time you get back up and get back in the ring you grow stronger. And YOWE grows weaker.

How much fight is in your dog?

12 THINGS YOU NEED TO KNOW ABOUT COURAGE

"Courage is a moral quality; it is not a chance gift of nature like an aptitude for games. It is a cold choice between two alternatives, the fixed resolve not to quit; an act of renunciation which must be made not once but many times by the power of will."

Lord Moran: The Anatomy of Courage: The Classic Study
of the Soldier's Struggle Against Fear

Courage is required to achieve your goals and dreams, and to become the person you are meant to be. Here are 12 things you should know about courage:

1. Fear is a liar that misrepresents reality; fear is a prison that holds you back more powerfully than iron bars; and fear is a thief that robs you of your peace and your potential. Fear will never tell you the truth. Fear wants you to be weak, because then it can be strong. By accepting fear's picture of a bleak future, you become a participant in a fraud – a fraud in which you are also the victim. To conquer this cowardly liar, you must confront it with strength and determination, and with the hope that it wishes to hide from you in the fog of despair.

2. Fear is a reaction, courage is a decision; perseverance is making that decision day after day after day.

3. Courage is not fearlessness. The absence of fear is not courage – the absence of fear is brain damage. No fear, no courage – big fear, big courage.

4. Courage is not an emotion, it is an action; people who do courageous things are not feeling courage, they are feeling fear and acting in spite of it.

5. Caring is the root of courage; when you care enough about something you will find the courage to do what needs to be done.

6. Low self-esteem is often just an excuse for cowardice. The abusive voice in the back of your head wants to prevent you from taking risks and taking action. To achieve your goals and become the person you are meant to be, you must rewrite that inner dialogue.

7. Courage without energy is just a good intention; energy without courage is more likely to run away than it is to stand and fight.

8. Give fear a name and it becomes just a problem – it's easier to solve problems than it is to conquer nameless fear.

9. The only way to escape from the prison of fear is action. You cannot wish your way out, you cannot wait your way out. You can only work your way out. Every time you escape the prison of fear, you grow stronger and more confident. It will always be there, trying to wall you in, but you will eventually grow so strong that you can just step right over the walls.

10. Fear wants to keep out anyone who's different, who makes you feel the least bit uncomfortable, anyone who challenges your established opinions and assumptions. At the same time that your fear is excluding them, their fear is excluding you. Pretty soon, they're not just different, they're worse. And of course, you're not just different to them, you're worse, too. And it's not a very big step from being worse to being wrong. And from being wrong it's not a very big step to being an enemy. Fear excludes and creates enemies. It takes courage to

bring down the walls of exclusion and reach out to people who are different from you.

11. Fear is many tomorrows, courage is one today. Fear is worrying about all the bad things that might happen in all the different tomorrows that your darkest imaginings will dredge up. Fear is worrying about the bad days that may or may not come, and even worrying about the good days because you know they can't last. You can dream of the future, plan for it – those are good things to do – but you can't control all the tomorrows. What you can do is tend to the work that is right in front of you today.

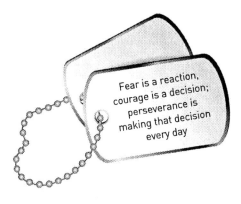

Fear is a reaction, courage is a decision; perseverance is making that decision every day

12. Don't get crushed between the anvil of yesterday's regrets and the hammer of tomorrow's worries. Define your future by your hopes and not by your fears, by your dreams and not by your memories.

MAKE THE MOST OF A GOOD SCARE

"A good scare is usually worth more than good advice."

Murphy's Law of Combat

You've no doubt read about how important it is to eat a healthy diet, get enough sleep, and exercise regularly, but if you're like most people you assume that advice doesn't apply to you. Until your doctor tells you that you are at high risk for dying of a heart attack.

You've seen the statistics that nine out of ten Americans have not adequately saved for retirement but you keep on spending every dollar you make. Until a financial planner calculates that you will run out of money twenty years before the end of your life expectancy.

A good scare can do one of the two things: It can paralyze you or it can catalyze you. Denial, rationalization, and procrastination are the weapons that YOWE uses to freeze you into inaction.

Facing reality and accepting the facts as they are and not as you wish they would be; replacing excuses with execution; and instilling in yourself a spirit of urgency – these are the weapons with which you stage your counterattack against YOWE.

COURAGE MEANS ACTING WITHOUT A GUARANTEE OF SUCCESS

When Mexican general Santa Anna surrounded Colonel William Travis and his small garrison at the Alamo in 1836, he sent Travis a note saying, in effect, "Surrender or die." Travis called his men down into the courtyard and challenged them to stay and fight for an independent Texas. To a man they did so, and for the next 13 days they held off a Mexican force that outnumbered them more than ten-to-one. On the day of the final Mexican assault, every single defender died fighting.

When 108 years later American general Anthony McAuliffe received a similar ultimatum from a German general at the Battle of the Bulge, he simply scribbled the word "Nuts!" across the bottom of the surrender demand and sent it back to the baffled German. Nearly surrounded and outnumbered, the American troops held off the Germans until they were relieved by General Patton's army, their courage having secured a pivotal victory.

Travis at the Alamo and McAuliffe at Bastogne shared one thing in common: uncertainty. Travis had no way of knowing that Sam Houston *would not be* successful at raising an army fast enough to break Santa Anna's siege of the Alamo; McAuliffe had no way of knowing that George Patton *would be* successful at turning his army 90-degrees on its heels and fighting his way through the dense Ardennes forest to relieve the 101st Airborne at Bastogne.

But each man knew what had to be done, even without being assured of success or survival. That is as good a definition of courage as you will find. I previously mentioned Norman Dixon's study on the psychology of military incompetence in which he found one common distinction between highly capable commanders and their inept counterparts: the latter had not developed the capacity to manage their anxiety. Uncontrolled anxiety can cause disastrous military blunders by inducing paralysis (as in the British failure to respond to the Japanese threat to Singapore early in World War Two) or panic (as in the desperation of Picket's Charge on the third and final day of the battle of Gettysburg).

It takes courage to chart your own path, to set audacious goals where success is uncertain, and to overcome the doubts and fears that stop those who are less courageous dead in their tracks. Amelia Earhart said that courage is the price life exacts for granting peace. It is also the price that a tough and competitive world demands for granting success.

The difference between courageous and crazy is evident only in retrospect

One more thing: The difference between courageous and crazy is often evident only long after the fact. The people who call you crazy for quitting a steady job to start your own company today will be the ones who in the future say "I knew her when..." after your picture has graced the cover of *Inc.* magazine.

MAKE FEAR YOUR ALLY, NOT YOUR ENEMY

In Herman Melville's novel *Moby Dick* first mate Starbuck said that a fearless man is more dangerous than a coward, because a fearless man is more likely to take crazy risks. The wise man acknowledges fear and uses it to his advantage. In this sense, fear can be an ally that prevents such risks. Fear is an ally when it draws your attention to critical problems in your work and in your life, and then impels you to take corrective action. Following are some of the steps to make fear work for you rather than against you:

» *Understand your fear:* What is it trying to tell you? Generally, fear can be trying to tell you that you are not ready for something that could soon happen, or that in some way you are on the wrong path in your life.

» *Talk back to your fear:* When fear is trying to prevent you from taking risks that could in fact eliminate the source of the fear, you need to put on your bravest face, rebut your fears with your bravest affirmations, then fake it till you make it (or fake it till you become it).

» *Get the facts:* Fear breeds in ignorance and dissipates when you shine the light of knowledge upon it. What do you not know now that if you did know would make your fear more manageable, and how can you find it out?

» *Prepare yourself:* Fear is often simply the suspicion that you are not ready for some future occurrence. What steps can take to prepare yourself for the future eventualities you fear today? Fear doesn't stand a chance when confronted with preparation and discipline.

» *Transform inertia into energy:* By altering your conscious perception of the emotion, you can transform paralyzing inertia of fear into catalyzing energy for action and change. The physiological symptoms of terror and exhilaration are identical – the only difference is the name that you give to the symptoms.

» *Pay attention:* Learn from the past, plan for the future, but live in the present. Fear is caused by dragging around the dead weight of past defeats and imagining more such defeats in the future. The antidote to this fear is present awareness, which can be cultivated through a disciplined practice of mindfulness.

» *Take action.* Do the thing you fear, said Ralph Waldo Emerson, and the death of the fear is certain. This ancient wisdom has never been more relevant than in today's fast-moving world. Action is the difference between wishful thinking and positive thinking. Action is the hacksaw that cuts through the prison bars of fear.

» *Connect with other people:* Speaking with others can give you comfort and courage, and might open your eyes to possibilities that you haven't yet considered for eliminating the source of your fears.

» *Have fun:* You cannot simultaneously be amused and frightened. Spontaneity, humor and laughter bolster courage. As a side benefit, they also foster creativity, fellowship, and joy. Oh, and if that's not reason enough, recent research shows that laughter and joy will make you healthier and help you live longer.

BE A VISIONARY, NOT A VICTIM

"As he had so many times before, Lincoln withstood the storm of defeat by replacing anguish over an unchangeable past with hope in an unchartered future."

Doris Kearns Goodwin: *Team of Rivals:*
The Political Genius of Abraham Lincoln.

Victims live in the past, dragging around the dead weight of ancient drama/trauma that holds them back from achieving their goals.

Visionaries live in the future, inspired by dreams that motivate them to do the work needed to achieve their dreams

Be a visionary, not a victim. Define your future by your hopes and not your fears, by your dreams and not your memories.

Define your future by your hopes and not by your fears, by your dreams and not by your memories

RESOLVE TO SPREAD COURAGE – EVEN IF YOU DON'T FEEL COURAGEOUS

Keep your fears to yourself, but share your courage with others. That was the excellent advice of Robert Louis Stevenson. Shortly after the 9/11 terrorist attacks I listened to a radio interview with a psychiatrist who specializes in working with corporate executives. The interviewer asked him which emotions a CEO should share with employees during times of crisis. All of them, the doctor replied, with the exception of fear. Fear is contagious, fear is malignant, and it's the leader's (and the parent's) responsibility to keep it in check.

In the movie *U-571*, an American submarine crew sets out to hijack a German U-boat, but everything goes awry. The American captain is killed, leaving his executive officer, Lieutenant Tyler, in command of a skeleton crew on a German submarine they do not know how to operate. Tyler honestly tells the men that he doesn't know how he'll get them out of the mess.

Later, Chief Klough, the old salt who's been in submarines since the new skipper was in diapers, comes into Tyler's quarters and gives the young lieutenant a royal chewing out, concluding by saying: "You're the skipper now, and the skipper *always* knows – even when he doesn't know, the skipper always knows." That's a pretty good metaphor for the responsibility of a leader, or a parent, in troubled times. You might not know what you're going to do, but you must believe in your ability to do *something*. More important, you must make your followers, or your children, believe that *you are capable of doing something*, and reassure them that whatever you decide to do will save the day.

In *Profiles in Courage* John F. Kennedy wrote: "To be courageous... requires no exceptional qualifications, no magic formula, no special combination of time, place and circumstance. It is an opportunity that sooner or later is presented to us all."

YOWE will want you to turn down that opportunity. YOWE will want you to keep the job that's killing your soul rather than starting a business doing something you love. YOWE would rather have you play the role of martyr and victim than confronting those who abuse or take advantage of you. YOWE would rather have you watch some-

Keep your fears to yourself, share your courage with others

one else's "reality" show on television than to see you create a new reality of your own.

Keep those fears to yourself. Pump up your courage — then infect others with it. You will be astonished at what you can accomplish together.

ACT WITH AUDACITY

"The more boldness lends wings to the mind and the discernment, so much farther will they reach in their flight."

Carl von Clausewitz: *On War*

In his tract on "The Art of War" (attached as an appendix to Samuel B. Griffith's translation of the much better known *The Art of War* by Sun Tzu) Wu Ch'i said: "Now the field of battle is a land of standing corpses; those determined to die [with glory] will live; those who hope to escape with their lives will die."

The individual who attacks life with passion, who finds work he loves and does that work with great passion and joy, and in the process creates real value for those he serves, has a high chance of surviving on "the field of battle." But the person who hangs onto a job he despises, hoping against hope to someday retire with an intact 401(k), dies a little bit more every day; while he might win a battle or two, he will eventually lose the war that matters most.

It's been said that no boat ever reached a distant shore without first leaving sight of the coastline. The uncertainty can be frightening – but it can also be exhilarating. As T.S. Eliot said, no one knows how far they can go without first running the risk of going too far.

YOWE IS JUST AS AFRAID OF YOU . . .

. . . as you are of it. In his memoires, Ulysses S. Grant wrote about how in 1861 he had been ordered to move upon a Confederate encampment on the far side of a hill. As they approached the top of the hill from which they expected to see the Rebels, possibly already formed up for battle, he became increasingly anxious. But upon reaching the crest of the hill he discovered that the enemy had abandoned their camp. That was, he said, a turning point for him. "From that event to the close of the war," he wrote, "I never experienced trepidation upon confronting an enemy... I never forgot that he had as much reason to fear my forces as I had his. It was a valuable lesson."

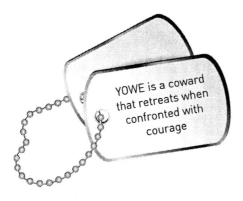

YOWE is a coward that retreats when confronted with courage

And it is a lesson that you should take to heart yourself. Shine a light on YOWE – don't let it slink around up there in the dark corners of your mind spraying the walls with the graffiti of negative self-talk. Stand up to YOWE with courage and determination and it will retreat like the cowardly bully it is.

MAKE SURE YOU'RE AFRAID OF THE RIGHT THINGS

If you read transcripts of Winston Churchill's most well-known speeches of World War II there is one message that you will *not* see: Churchill never told his countrymen to not be afraid. He promised them toil, blood, sweat and tears but he never promised them fear-lessness. He knew they were afraid, that they had good reason to be afraid, and didn't jeopardize his credibility by trying to convince them otherwise. Rather, he strove to make sure that they were afraid of the right things – losing a war to Germany and becoming enslaved.

Total quality management guru W. Edwards Deming made "drive fear out of the workplace" one of his 14 points for TQM for the very good reason that frightened people are not particularly creative, responsive, or willing to stop the assembly line (literally and figuratively) when there is a quality problem. But as psychiatrist Scott Peck noted in *The Road Less Traveled*, the absence of fear is not courage – the absence of fear is brain damage! How do we reconcile those two concepts?

The answer is to make sure that people are afraid of the right things. If an employee is more afraid of the boss than of the competition, then the competition will eventually win. If you are more afraid of being rejected than you are of seeing your business fail or your book never being published, then being afraid of the wrong things will ineluctably bring about a self-fulfilling prophecy of failure.

In their book *Nuts! Southwest Airlines' Crazy Recipe for Business and Personal Success*, Kevin and Jackie Freiberg tell the story of how in 1994 Southwest responded to the launch by (at the time much larger) United Airlines of their United Shuttle. This was an arrow aimed directly at the heart of Southwest. Then-CEO Herb Kelleher sent a letter to all Southwest employees entitled "Commencement of Hostilities" that quoted Churchill and called upon the "martial vigor" of his people for the impending campaign. The Freiberg's book includes a photograph of a woman working in a Southwest reservation center in full combat regalia.

Kelleher knew that he could not "drive fear out of the workplace." If he'd told his people to not worry about the United assault, they would have wondered what he'd been drinking and their anxiety would have gone into overdrive. Kelleher's genius was to make sure that his people were afraid of the right thing – losing customers to United Shuttle – and not the wrong thing – the possibility that they could lose their jobs. The implicit message was that if they all did their jobs, no one would have to worry about losing their jobs. Today United Shuttle is

Make sure that people are afraid of the right things

a speck in the dustbin of history and Southwest is flying higher than ever with the most loyal workforce in the industry.

Psychologists tell us that the most paralyzing of all fears is not the fear of failure – it's the fear of success. That fear lies at the root of much self-sabotaging behav-

ior; it is one of YOWE's most potent weapons. We tend to resist that which we're afraid of. If you are truly afraid of failure, you will fight like hell to prevent it from happening. If you are afraid of success, then you will find excuses to not do the things that are necessary for you to be successful. The biggest problems come for people who think they are afraid of failure when what they are really afraid of is success.

DARE MOST WHEN TIMES ARE DARKEST

Sherman: Well, Grant, we've had the devil's own day, haven't we?
Grant: Yes. Yes. Lick 'em tomorrow though.

On April 6, 1862 the Confederate army launched a surprise attack on Union forces at Shiloh and badly mauled the Yankees. That night, as his men huddled without shelter in a drenching rain, William Tecumseh Sherman met with his commander, Ulysses S. Grant, expecting to be given the order to retreat. Instead Grant – the man President Abraham Lincoln said he could not afford to lose "because he fights" – ordered a counterattack on the following morning. All lost ground was retaken and what had appeared to be a certain defeat was turned into a stunning Union Victory.

It's often during what seems to be the darkest of times that the greatest opportunities show up right there in front of us if we have the courage and the endurance to give one more push. It takes courage to start a business after you've been laid off from the day job. It takes perseverance to pull out a fresh yellow pad or fire up a laptop to start a new novel after having just received your 49th rejection letter for the last novel.

Remember: The 23rd Psalm does not say "Yea though I take up permanent residence in the valley of the shadow." Oh, to be sure, you can choose to pitch a tent – or buy a condo – and spend the rest of your life down there in the shadows of hopeless despair. But if you keep walking, if you keep hammering away, if the morning after the day of your most devastating loss you can find the courage to once again take the fight to the enemy, you too just might transform apparent defeat into stunning victory.

KNOW WHEN YOU HAVE NO CHOICE BUT TO STICK YOUR NECK OUT

In *Strategy: The Logic of War and Peace* Edward N. Luttwak describes how armies that have a significant advantage of men and material can afford to attack cautiously across a broad front, while those at a significant disadvantage and thus already at risk must take even more risk by attacking boldly if they are to have any chance of success. The nation with a large army can fight the war of the 800-pound gorilla, as did the United Stated during the Vietnam War, where the Americans sought to defend everywhere and attack across a broad front. The nation with a numerically inferior military must fight the war of the guerrilla, audaciously attacking their enemies with tightly concentrated objectives – the sort of war successfully carried out by the North Vietnamese.

The risks of audacity are often lower than the risks of timidity

The individual who is independently wealthy can afford to let his or her money sit in a mutual fund account while they play golf every day. The 60-year old who hasn't even started saving for retirement cannot afford this cautious, conservative approach. He or she must take on a second job, work lots of overtime, slash spending to the barest essentials, and invest much more aggressively to have any chance of a comfortable retirement.

The owner of a mom-and-pop grocery store cannot respond to the opening of a new Super Walmart right across the street by running coupon ads in the local paper. To survive, much less thrive, she must fight the war of the guerrilla, audaciously attacking the giant where it is weakest and establishing a sustainable source of competitive advantage in a narrow area that can realistically be defended.

UNDERSTAND THE LAWS OF ADVERSITY

The first American offensive operation in World War II was the battle at Kasserine Pass in North Africa. It was a disaster. But the lessons learned from that disaster were invaluable in preparing for future success in the invasions of Sicily and Normandy. Adversity is bitter medicine but it can make us stronger. As the Arab proverb puts it, all sunshine makes a desert (and with the rain comes flowers and rainbows). Without adversity, there would be no need for perseverance – but with perseverance, adversity becomes an opportunity for personal growth. And here are its laws:

> » *Law #1:* The rain will fall on the just and the unjust alike, and bad things will happen to good people – including you. Understand that adversity will come and be ready to welcome it when it does for the lessons it will bring, for the strength and wisdom you will gain from it, and for the people it can bring into your life. And refuse to play the victim role when it strikes.

> » *Law #2:* You must pass through the valley of the shadow, but you don't have to take up permanent residence in the cold darkness. Life is a motion picture, not a snapshot - your trajectory is more important than your current position. As Winston Churchill said, if you're going through hell – keep going!

> » *Law #3:* Whether it's the best of times or the worst of times is defined by what you choose to see. Without the valleys, you won't appreciate the mountains, and there are millions of others who would *love* to have your problems, whatever they are.

» *Law #4:* One door closes, another door opens. There is opportunity hidden in every adversity if you have the strength and courage to search for it and to pursue it when you've found it.

» *Law #5:* Falling on your face is good for your head. We learn and grow more from our setbacks than we do from our successes. When things aren't working, it forces you to look at more creative solutions.

» *Law #6:* Surviving adversity is a great way to build self-confidence, and to give you a more positive perspective on future adversity (if we survived that we can survive anything!). Adversity toughens you and prepares you for bigger challenges and accomplishments in the future.

» *Law #7:* What you've fought to gain you'll fight to keep and vice versa – easy come, easy go. What you had to fight hard to gain you will fight doubly hard to retain.

» *Law #8:* When you respond to adversity by playing the role of victim or martyr, you weaken your character – and that weakness makes it virtually certain that you will attract even more adversity in the future. To play the victim is to invite being victimized.

» *Law #9:* Adversity is an antidote for hubris, arrogance, and complacency. When you are flat on your back you have no choice but to ask for help in getting back up. And it is often when you are flat on your back that you meet the people who mean the most to you (something many support group participants experience firsthand).

» *Law #10:* You will learn to help someone else who has bigger problems than you do. Whatever you most need in life, the best way for you to get it is to help someone else get it who needs it more than you do.

» *Law #11:* Adversity keeps teaching – it provides great stories for the grandchildren! Your setbacks can, if you're committed to learning from them and teaching about them, be the source of great learning for others.

» *Law #12:* Every great accomplishment was once the "impossible" dream of a dreamer who refused to quit when the going got tough.

Saturday's promise from The Self Empowerment Pledge, which we'll get into in Part 3, says: "Though I might not understand why adversity happens, by my conscious choice I will find strength, compassion, and grace through my trials." That is an excellent formula for making the adversity of today the platform for success and accomplishment tomorrow.

Every great accomplishment was once the "impossible" dream of a dreamer who refused to quit

PLOW THROUGH THE PAIN

On the morning of May 7, 1492 – nearly 80 years into The 100 Years War – Joan of Arc led French forces in an attack against the English stronghold of Les Tourelles in the city of Orleans. While holding her banner at the front lines she was hit by an arrow in the shoulder. Joan was taken from the battlefield for care, but returned later that day to encourage her men as they once again stormed the fortress. The English were driven from Orleans the next day, and this was widely seen as the sign Joan had promised for a turning point in the war. Over the coming months she led French forces to victory after victory, suffering several more wounds along the way. She was eventually captured and burned at the stake, but not before changing the course of history.

Joseph Campbell, student and author on the meaning of myth, defined the hero's journey – a journey he said we are all called upon to make in our own lives. At one point in every hero's story the hero is thrown from his horse, loses his sword in the mud, and we want to cover our eyes as we see the dragon hovering over him breathing fire. This is, we fear, almost certainly the end. But somehow, the hero manages to find his sword, slay the dragon, remount the horse – then go on the rescue the beautiful princess and they live happily ever after.

An inevitable chapter in your own hero's journey will be facing the pain of rejection, failure, and defeat. The arrows that strike you are more likely to be metaphorical than real, but you will eventually be struck down just as surely as Joan was. Then the question will be whether you have the strength and the endurance to pick up the banner and soldier on. "Once more into the breach, dear friends!" Shakespeare had English King Henry V admonish his troops during the siege of Harfleur some 80 years before Joan rallied her countrymen.

In his beautiful book *The Last Lecture*, Randy Pausch wrote: "Brick walls are not there to stop you they are there to make you prove how much you want something." Whatever it is you want, you will run into brick walls. The bigger the goal the more and higher will be the walls.

The bigger your goal, the greater the challenges you will confront

How much do you want it? Are you willing to fight for it? Are you determined that, no matter how hard you fall, you will pick up your banner and charge once more into the breach?

One more thing: No matter how hard you fall, the worst that can happen is never really that bad. They can reject you but they cannot kill you; they can ridicule you but they cannot eat you. And I positively guarantee that no matter what else they might be able to do to you, they cannot burn you at the stake.

NEVER GIVE IN TO ANXIETY AND DEPRESSION

"Keep your spirits up, don't allow yourself to be depressed, and never for one moment doubt but that matters will finish better and more quickly than you imagine."

Napoleon Bonaparte in a letter to one of his generals

"We shall never surrender!" Anyone who doubts the power of words to change history should read about how the speeches of Sir Winston Churchill fortified the courage of the British people during the darkest days of World War II, when they stood alone against the evil empire of Nazi Germany. To all outward appearances, they were beaten. There was no way that the demoralized British Army, having only recently completed its humiliating evacuation from Dunkirk, could stand up to the German military juggernaut. And yet their refusal to surrender during those darkest days kept them fighting on until they were joined in the conflict by the United States and the Soviet Union, which preordained the eventual victory.

YOWE is by nature a quitter. When the going gets tough, YOWE wants you to go shopping or turn on the television. YOWE wants you to throw in the towel and try something else rather than persevere your way through the difficulties. YOWE hates frustration. But as Anthony Robbins says in his book *Awaken the Giant Within*, there are two sorts of people in the world – people who have worked their way through frustration and people who wish they had.

In *Finding Serenity in the Age of Anxiety* Robert Gerzon describes "the comfort zone" as being bounded by two walls: anxiety and depression. He says that it is human nature to become dissatisfied with the status quo. So we dream of something new – going back to school, starting a business, writing a book, changing the world.

But as we move toward actually doing something about that dream, we run into a wall of anxiety. What if it doesn't work? What if it turns out to have not been what we wanted after all? What if people whose opinions we care about don't approve? Once the anxiety becomes overwhelming, we quit and retreat back into the comfort zone. Only we overshoot and hit the wall on the other side: depression. We get depressed because now we feel like a quitter, or a failure. We know that having quit once, having failed once, it will be all that much harder to motivate ourselves to try again.

Never allow anxiety or depression to be an excuse for not trying

Anxiety and depression are two of YOWE's weapons for keeping you paralyzed, firmly entrenched in the misery of a comfort zone, the emotional basket covering the candle of your meant-to-be-brilliance. In *Too Soon Old, Too Late Smart* psychiatrist (and Vietnam veteran) Gordon Livingston writes that medication can relieve the symptoms of anxiety and depression, but medication cannot make you happy. Only action can do that. To defeat YOWE you must never allow anxiety or depression to be your excuse for not trying in the first place or for quitting once you have started.

BOUNCE BACK FROM EVERY SETBACK BUT KNOW WHEN TO BOUNCE BACK ALONG A NEW VECTOR

After the first day of fighting in the Wilderness Campaign, defeated Union troops were marching to the rear in anticipation of the retreat that had been ordered by every previous Federal commander who had been whipped by Robert E. Lee. There on a horse at the crossroads sat the new commander of the northern armies, Ulysses S. Grant, waving the column off to the right – to prepare for the next day's attack on Lee's flank. Grant's resolve to take the fight to Lee along a new vector rather than to turn tail and run or, worse yet, attack along the same line that had been such a disaster the day before, had an instantaneously galvanizing impact upon the morale of the troops.

Almost everyone who has lost a job feels terrible in the immediate aftermath, but eventually is able to proclaim that it was the best thing that could have happened. The personal commitment to always "bounce back" will shorten the painful interval between encountering a setback and finding its hidden blessings. Sometimes, though, this will mean bouncing back along a new vector. A substantial number of new businesses, as just one example, are started by people who have lost jobs and decided to take a new direction with their lives rather than seeking another job doing what they have done in the past. Think about the adversity you most fear; if it were to happen, what are some possible alternative "bounce-back" vectors you could follow?

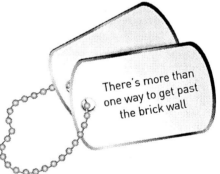

There's more than one way to get past the brick wall

YOU ALMOST NEVER "CAN'T"

The book *Impossible Victories* by Bryan Perrett describes ten battles in which the victors overcame incredible disadvantages to prevail over an enemy force that in many cases was larger, better equipped, and more advantageously positioned. In each case, Perrett wrote, "the one factor present in all was the will to win, at all costs."

One of the key turning points of World War Two was the battle of Stalingrad. On August 23, 1942 German bombers turned that city into a deadly inferno. In the coming months, the *Wehrmacht* drove Russian defenders back into a tiny enclave of the devastated city where, with their backs to the Volga, they clawed and scratched to keep their toehold in a few shattered factory buildings. Stalin declared that under no circumstances was the city bearing his name to fall. With a superhuman effort under atrocious circumstances the Red Army held on, grinding down the German Sixth Army and setting it up for the knock-out punch delivered that winter when General Zhukov executed a double envelopment far to the German rear.

The victory assured Russia's survival, and was the beginning of the end of the Nazi army's offensive power. The cost was enormous: during the five month battle the Red Army suffered over one million casualties, including nearly half-a-million dead (more than the United States lost in every theatre during the entire war). During the darkest days of the battle, the average life expectancy of a Soviet soldier was less than two days. Russian determination, and the concomitant willingness to pay the steep price for victory, transformed the shape of the war and set the stage for ultimate victory. The primary difference between winners and also-rans is often simply that winners refuse to quit, even when to all outside appearances the battle has been lost.

When I hike in the Grand Canyon, I occasionally encounter a hiker at the bottom who looks at the steep and long path to the top and wails

"I can't!" They have convinced themselves that there's no way they can hike out of The Canyon. Their feet are blistered, their knees ache, their pack is too heavy, there are a thousand reasons why they "can't" make it under their own power. Trust me, though, there is not a refugee camp at the bottom of the Grand Canyon for all the hikers who made it down but could not make it back out. They all eventually find the strength for the march out.

That is a pretty good metaphor for one of YOWE's favorite tricks – trying to convince you that you "can't" do something. Because once you're convinced that you can't do it, you won't even try. Then YOWE knows it's won. If you're convinced you can't do something difficult and demanding (like hiking the Grand Canyon), then you'll probably settle for something that's easy and mindless – like seeing Grand Canyon from a bus window while en route to Las Vegas, that global capitol of mindless self-indulgence.

You never "can't" – you only "can't yet"

Any time you catch yourself uttering those toxic two words "I can't" remind yourself that it's probably not true. What you're really saying is that you don't want to, that it would be difficult or expensive, or that there are other things that you would rather do. So when you hear that disempowering word come out of your mouth, instantly add the word "yet." When you say "I can't yet," what you are really saying is "I can, but first I need to (fill in the blank – save more money, get in shape, get more information, whatever).

When you append the word "yet" to "I can't" you shift your focus from the past – all the reasons you are stuck – to the future – all the things you must do in order to remove the letter "t" from the word "can."

COUPLE "IMPOSSIBLE" GOALS WITH "IMPOSSIBLE" DEADLINES TO CREATE A SENSE OF URGENCY

In the years following World War I, America's military languished in the back waters of the Great Depression. When Hitler invaded Poland in 1939, the United States had the world's eighteenth largest army – and a woefully under-equipped army when compared with those of potential enemies. The economy was still in the doldrums of the Great Depression and assembly lines were still gathering dust and rust. Following the Japanese attack on Pearl Harbor and Hitler's subsequent declaration of war on the United States in 1941, the Roosevelt administration established one "impossible" goal after another and gave each one an "impossible" deadline, a pattern that was to persist throughout the war. They established "impossible" goals and "impossible" deadlines for quotas on weapons production, recruiting and training of soldiers, transport of supplies to allies, and invasion schedules.

Less than five years later, the United States stood victorious on every battlefield and possessed both the greatest military force and most powerful economy in the world.

Committing yourself to an "impossible" goal with an "impossible" deadline has a wonderful way of clarifying and focusing the mind on key priorities such as getting out of debt or breaking addictive behaviors. It's like the classic case of being enormously productive the day before you leave for vacation. Think about a goal that is very important to you, but which you have been putting off taking action to accomplish. Now, give yourself a deadline. Chances are, the only thing standing between you and the achievement of that big goal by that deadline is YOWE.

SEIZE OPPORTUNITY

In July of 1812, British and French forces were faced off near Salamanca in Spain. Duke Wellington – the Iron Duke who would later defeat Napoleon at Waterloo – was about to order his army to retreat back to Portugal when he saw a gap open up in the French lines. "By God, they are extending their lines," he shouted, "order my horses." He immediately ordered an attack. By the end of a hard-fought day it was the French who were in full retreat.

Every now and then life opens unexpected doors of opportunity – often at times when we are mentally and emotionally in retreat mode. A newly unemployed person suddenly has a chance to change careers or start a business. A cancer survivor is asked to speak in public about courage and perseverance, opening the door to what heretofore had been a fantasy about being a professional speaker. A new college graduate can't find a job in her discipline, forcing her to explore other options. She starts a business and several years later her company is featured in *Fast Company* magazine.

The first response to unexpected opportunity is almost always resistance to the idea. That is the voice of YOWE telling us that it's too risky, that it's not a good time, that we might fail – that we should give up the dream and get another job doing the same thing we were doing in the job we just lost, that we should stay home and regain our strength and let some other cancer survivor go out and make the speeches, that we should move back in with the parents and wait for the job market to improve.

While it's usually a good idea to think twice before taking a risk on something new, YOWE would have you think it to death by painting vivid mental pictures of every possible catastrophe that could result from making the leap. When I autograph a copy of my book *The Florence Prescription* I inscribe the words: Proceed Until Apprehended.

It's a powerful philosophy. If your attitude is to proceed on doing what needs to be done, and doing it now, you will get a lot more done. And if you proceed fast enough, by the time anyone else figures out what you're doing it will be too late to stop you! Besides, if you don't let YOWE stop you it's unlikely that anyone else will be able to.

Proceed
Until
Apprehended!

HAVE A "NO PROBLEM" MINDSET

"The difficult we do immediately. The impossible takes a little longer."

Motto of the U.S. Army Corps of Engineers during World War II

Auto-Owners Insurance Company is a 100-year old Fortune 500 company that was a Values Coach client for many years. They call themselves The "No Problem" People® and when working with the company those are two words one hears a lot – No Problem.

Now, when you tell a truculent teenager to go clean his room or mow the lawn and the response is "No problem," what he really means is probably some variation of "That's your problem, not mine – if you want the lawn mowed, go do it yourself."

Over the years of working with Auto-Owners I learned that when one of their associates says "No Problem" what they really mean is "I see you have a problem and I am going to take responsibility for fixing that problem for you so you don't need to worry about it anymore."

Same words – totally different meaning.

When you hear yourself saying "No Problem" in that first context – blowing it off – you can be pretty sure that YOWE is pulling the strings.

When you hear yourself saying "No Problem" in the second context – taking ownership for resolving the problem no matter how "impossible" it might seem at the time – you know it's the authentic you speaking, the you that is determined to achieve your goals regardless of the "problems" that crop up along the way.

Another way of knowing that it's the authentic you saying the words is that you'll probably hear YOWE shrieking that it's impossible. When that happens, remember that the impossible just takes a little longer. Then break the problem down into doable steps and immediately set about tackling the first step.

CONCENTRATE VITAL RESOURCES AT THE DECISIVE POINT OF ACTION

"When we turn pro, everything becomes simple... We now structure our hours not to flee from fear, but to confront it and overcome it. We plan our activities in order to accomplish an aim. And we bring all our will to bear so that we stick to this resolution."

Steven Pressfield: *Turning Pro*

"Concentration," wrote Ralph Waldo Emerson, "is the great secret of strength in politics, in war, in trade, in short in all management of human affairs." Napoleon was often outnumbered on the overall battlefield, but was able to win tactical victories by concentrating superior forces at the key point. This same principle of *Schwerpunkt* (focal point of attack) was the foundational doctrine of the German *Blitzkrieg* campaigns early in the Second World War.

After the battle of Guadalcanal, allied military leaders realized that if they had to fight like that to re-capture every Pacific island taken by the Japanese, it would cost years and ghastly casualties to reach Tokyo. They also realized that their goal was to end the war, not to recover every pile of rock that poked a forest-canopied nose above the waves. Thus was born the strategy of island-hopping. Only those islands were targeted that were critical to progress towards mainland Japan, and the entire might of air, land, and sea forces was brought down upon the defenders of those islands.

In *The 80/20 Principle: The Secret to Success by Achieving More With Less*, Richard Koch wrote: "The war is between the trivial many and the vital few." Here is an exercise to help you concentrate on those vital few. Go through your calendar for the last six months and use a colored highlighters to highlight activities directly related to helping you achieve your key priorities ("on target"). Count up the hours for each category.

If you're being honest with yourself, it's likely that you're going to find that 20% (or less) of your time and energy is being devoted to your key priorities (the vital few), and the other 80% is being expended on the "trivial many." Now, go back and look through your calendar for *the next* six months. There will obviously be blocks of time that *must* be kept on your calendar (e.g. scheduled meetings with the boss) and there will be blocks of time you'll *want* to keep on your calendar (e.g. the summer trip to Yosemite). Working around those givens, block off at least 5.6 hours during each week (that's 10% of seven 8-hour days) that you will *absolutely commit* to focusing on a key priority (such as preparing for graduate school, starting your new business, writing the great American novel, or taking your kids to the science museum).

In one of the first self-help books of the modern era (*Wake Up and Live!* published in 1936), Dorothea Brande wrote that failure to concentrate on key priorities actually constitutes "the will to fail." People have so many things going on that they cannot do or be their best at the things that really matter, but when they do fail, at least they will always have the excuse that they were too busy doing something else. What she describes is a human version of the old shell game performed by the circus con man. Multi-tasking is like a monstrous shell game in which YOWE is the con man constantly shifting your attention from one priority to another so rapidly that you are never able to concentrate and complete any one of them. The essence of true success relies on your ability to concentrate vital resources on key priorities, on what really matters.

I have a sign posted in my home office that says "The One Big Yes requires lots of little no's." It's a constant reminder that if I'm to achieve my goals then I must be willing to say no to all of the bright shiny objects one which YOWE will tempt me to waste my time and money.

Warning: YOWE *absolutely hates it* when you make commitments to yourself – especially the ones that aren't fun and that entail work, commitment, and sacrifice. So be prepared to face a storm of inner resistance.

THE DIRECTION DEFLECTION QUESTION (DDQ)

"Winners concentrate, losers don't, or not as well... To concentrate takes guts. Every time you concentrate {on a personal goal}, you're taking a gamble."

David J. Rogers: *Waging Business Warfare*

The Direction Deflection Question (DDQ) is a simple yet very effective method for you to change your attitudes, your habits, and your behaviors – and to keep you focused on your most important goals. With consistent use of DDQs, you can change the results you are getting in your work and in your life. The DDQ is a way of stopping yourself in your tracks for a personal reality check, and then changing your course of action. Here is the basic DDQ:

Will what I'm about to do or say help me be my ideal best self?

The DDQ is really three questions in one. The first question is this: Who am I when I'm being my best self (as a parent, as a professional, as a time and money manager, and as a person). You cannot know whether what you are about to do or say will help you be your best self if you haven't thought clearly about your ideal self-identity in its various dimensions.

The second question is whether what you are about to do or say will help you be that best self. You have to listen carefully for the voice of your authentic best self because YOWE will be much louder. When best self is whispering that you should get up early, YOWE will be screaming that you should sleep in, then go to the coffee shop and have a few donuts.

Assuming the answer to the second question is no (hint: if it's not "no" a lot more than it's "yes," you're probably not being honest with yourself), then the second question to ask is what would you be doing if you were acting as your best self (hint: if it's more difficult than what you were about to say or act upon, it's probably the right answer). If you can bring yourself to do that "best self" answer, you will act your way into being the person you want to be.

The DDQ is infinitely adaptable, and can be tailored to virtually any area of desired personal improvement. Here are several examples.

> » **Managing time:** Is what I am about to do with my next hour going to help me achieve the goal that most matters to me right now?

> » **Managing money:** Is what I'm about to spend my hard-earned cash on going to help me achieve my goal of having all credit card debt paid off by the end of the next year?

> » **Physical health:** Will what I'm about to put into my mouth help me achieve my desired body weight?

> » **Building relationships:** Will what I'm about to say to this (family member, friend, coworker, customer) be seen in a friendly, positive, and constructive manner?

What is one area of your life in which you would like to see changes made? Create a DDQ for that purpose. Post it where you will see it often. Write the letters "DDQ" on the back of your hand with a ball-point pen each morning as a reminder to keep asking yourself the questions. Do that often enough and you will begin to make the necessary changes to achieve your desired outcomes and work your way toward being that best self.

DON'T PICK FIGHTS YOU DON'T NEED TO FIGHT

In the early 13th century, the Shah of Khwarazm abetted the murder of ambassadors who had been sent to him by Mongol warlord Genghis Khan, thus picking a fight he did not need to fight, and one that he could not afford to lose – though lose he did, bringing down upon his people a catastrophe of enormous proportions; Khwarazm and its entire population disappeared from the face of the globe.

I once pulled out onto a country road in front of a pickup truck hauling a big trailer full of hay bales that was lumbering along at a fraction of the speed limit. I thought I had plenty of space, but the driver of the truck obviously did not. As soon as I pulled out he hit the accelerator and very nearly crashed into my rear end. For the next several miles he tailgated me with his hand on the horn, and when I turned off he gave me a few choice profanities and a middle finger.

Whose day do you think was ruined, mine or his? His anger not only didn't bother me, it gave me something to laugh about. He, on the other hand, ruined what should have been a great start to a beautiful day, and in all likelihood took that anger to work and told anyone who would listen about the jerk he thought had cut him off in traffic. In effect, this man picked a fight he did not need to fight. The only harm done was that he might have had to slow down by a few miles per hour and be a few seconds later to work, but he reacted as though I had insulted his wife and kicked his dog. This jolt of negative energy might well have set the tone for the rest of his day. Even worse, in all likelihood it was the first thing he dumped on his family when he got home that evening.

I have a friend who has fiercely-held opinions on everything, and who as a consequence is almost always angry. He issues forth a constant stream of letters to editors, letters to policy-makers, letters to total strangers about everything from global warming to the deficiencies of political candidates. On the rare occasions when he actually gets a response, it's almost always a form letter. But his sense of righteous indignation has been stoked. Unfortunately, all the time he puts into drafting and redrafting those angry unanswered letters have prevented him from getting a start on the book he's always said he's going to write – someday.

YOWE loves these unnecessary little declarations of emotional war, because not only do they distract you from getting any real work done, they allow you to wallow around in a state

Don't waste time and energy on fights in which there is no possible victory

of righteous self-indignation and martyrdom. And when you lose these unnecessary little fights (as you inevitably will) they become YOWE's justification for making sure that you see one of life's pathetic victims looking back at you from the mirror every morning.

WINNING THE WAR WITH YOURSELF

ATTACK AT THE DECISIVE POINT WITH CONVERGING WAVES OF ASSAULT

William Tecumseh Sherman kept his enemies "on the horns of a dilemma" by marching in widely separated columns which could be converged upon the target of his choosing (or in the more expressive if less elegant phrase of George Patton, he could "hold 'em by the nose and kick 'em in the ass").

The alcoholic struggling to gain sobriety is practicing this strategy when he joins AA *and* sees a counselor *and* signs up for the health club *and* begins to change his circle of friends *and* works to reconcile with old friends and family members.

If you find yourself in "poor me" mode playing the part of victim, you can be sure that YOWE is at work. You can hold YOWE by the nose and kick it in the ass by taking complete responsibility for your finances *and* turning off the television and picking up a book that educates and inspires *and* committing yourself to at least 30 minutes of physical exercise at least five times a week *and* joining a service club where you can make a commitment to creating a better world rather than whining about how unfairly the world has treated you.

Do this and you will keep YOWE on the horns of a dilemma; you'll hit it from so many different directions it won't know which way to turn. You'll have it trying to defend everywhere all at once – and as Frederick the Great said, to defend everywhere is to defend nowhere.

COMMIT TO DAILY PRACTICE

"Habit gives strength to the body in great exertion, to the mind in great danger, to the judgment against first impressions."

Carl Von Clausewitz: *On War*

In *The War of Art* Steve Pressfield calls it turning pro. To turn pro doesn't necessarily mean that you get paid for the work or that you have joined a profession. It means that every day you pick up your lunch pail, put on your hard hat, and do your work. It means that you cultivate the habits, the rituals, and the disciplines that will be necessary for you to achieve your goals. Pressfield says, "Resistance hates it when we turn pro."

Solid habits are both a sword and shield in the war against YOWE

If you are only committed when it's easy and convenient, are easily distracted by bright shiny objects, and only do the work when you feel like it, then YOWE will defeat you every time. But when you develop the strength of habit, YOWE doesn't stand a chance.

If you want to achieve financial independence, you must cultivate the habit of automatically saving a portion of your income – no exceptions.

If you want to run a marathon, you must cultivate the habit of training every day – no exceptions.

If you want to write a book, you must cultivate the habit of writing every day – no exceptions.

If you want to lose weight you must cultivate the habit of eating less and exercising more – no exceptions.

If you want to be positive, energized, and determined in doing your work, you must cultivate the habit of getting enough sleep at night – no exceptions.

A web of solid habits is both a shield and sword in the war against YOWE. It is the shield that protects you from giving in to negative

A web of solid habits is shield and sword in the war against YOWE

self-talk, laziness and procrastination. And it is the sword that allows you to attack anxiety and fear, self-limiting beliefs and self-imposed limitations, and plow your way through the obstacles and setbacks that inevitably stand between you and the goals that are most important to you.

MAINTAIN YOUR MOBILITY

The army that stands behind defensive barricades, said Napoleon, is a beaten army. From the campaigns of Alexander the Great to Sherman's march to the sea and Patton's race to the Rhine, mobility has been a hallmark of military success. Even the young foot soldier in *The Red Badge of Courage*, Stephen Crane's novel of the Civil War, recognized that "it would be death to stay in the present place," and that the only safety lay in attacking and dislodging the enemy.

Mental mobility is more important than physical mobility

In almost every case, mental mobility precedes, and is more important than, physical mobility. As transient as we believe our society to be, far too many of us are immobilized by our fears and doubts; are unwilling to make the trade-off between geographic and professional mobility; and continue ramming headlong into life's brick walls rather than finding a way around them. Understanding the following factors can help you maintain your mobility, and the life and work options that such mobility can give you:

1. There is a common misperception that people are afraid of change (no one likes change but a wet baby!), but that's frankly not true. People *love* change – as long as it's change that comes with the guarantee of a positive outcome (nobody will complain if you change their paycheck by adding a zero to the dollar amount with no strings attached). Since none of us can guarantee that change will be for the better, we

must cultivate the mental capacity to deal with the anxiety of uncertainty, and help others at home and work do the same.

2. Everyone experiences misery of one sort or another. You must eventually choose between the certainty of misery or the misery of uncertainty.

3. *Never Quit* does not mean "don't stop." If something is not working, by all means stop. What it does mean is don't give up – on yourself and on your dreams. Sometimes the best way to assure that you don't *quit* is to *stop* doing something that isn't working, to redirect your energies into more productive channels.

4. The more "stuff" you haul around in the backpack of your life, the harder it will be for you to be quick and nimble.

WHEN THE HORSE IS DEAD, GET OFF

In his book *A Storm in Flanders* about the 4-year long stalemate of the Ypres Salient during World War I, Winston Groom asks why the British military doomed so many thousands of men to suffer and die in muddy trenches by hanging on to a strategically worthless and militarily disadvantageous piece of ground, when every 18-year-old conscript could see the stupidity of not pulling back to straighten their line and pull their men out of such a hideously exposed position. The answer, he concluded, was that it was "too bitter a pill

If what you're doing now isn't working – stop!

to swallow" to be seen to retreat and give in to "the Huns." The decision was psychological and emotional, not strategic and rational. Tens of thousands of men paid for that bitter pill with their lives.

If what you are doing now isn't working, stop! Be willing to take one step back so that you can take two steps forward. If the horse is dead, get off!

The challenge, of course, is knowing whether the horse is really dead or just needs a few more jabs of the spurs to get it moving. In my experience, the best test is to ask yourself how you would feel if you got off.

If you'd imagine a liberating sense of relief, a renewed burst of energy for new projects or a new direction, it's probably time to redirect.

On the other hand, if you'd feel disappointed and let down, and like you had disappointed and let down others, then you probably need to soldier on.

You have to be nimble, you have to be quick, if you want to jump over the candlestick.

START FAST, FINISH STRONG

"Rapidity is the essence of war: take advantage of the enemy's unreadiness, make your way by unexpected routes, and attack unguarded spots."

Sun Tzu: The Art of War

One of the things that made Napoleon's armies so formidable was that they marched at a cadence of 120 steps per minute (try that yourself for twenty miles or so and you'll be impressed!) when the standard of the day was only 70 paces per minute. As a result, they often showed up where they were not expected, and when they attacked an enemy line they hit with extraordinary force. Napoleon also recognized that victory would, as he put it, go to the army with the last reserves to throw into the battle. He knew that the secret of success was to start fast and finish strong.

Start Fast, Finish Strong is the motto of my friend Gary Ryan Blair, creator of The 100 Day Challenge. Success loves speed, Gary says, but

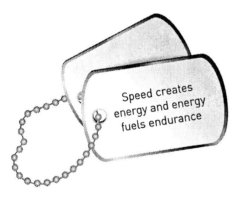

Speed creates energy and energy fuels endurance

you must also have the endurance to keep it up past the finish line.

Start fast. Double time yourself. Make a list of all the chores you have to do: grocery shopping, laundry, mowing the yard, etc. Now, figure out how you can do each of these in half the time.

With grocery shopping, for example, you can have a better organized list, refuse to engage in impulse buying or comparison shopping (since your time is more valuable than the modest amount of money you might save), and push your cart more decisively down the aisles.

This will give you a double benefit. By moving faster, you will be more energetic. You'll also have more time in which to invest that extra energy into more productive and enjoyable activities (hopefully, you do not consider shopping to be one of your more productive and enjoyable activities!).

Finish strong. Instead of relaxing in front of the tube at the end of the day, spend an extra hour on the treadmill, or reading a good book. Or both at once. Simultaneously exercising and reading is one of the very few instances where multitasking really can work.

MENTAL MOBILITY IS ESSENTIAL TODAY

Any idiot can order a frontal assault against an enemy line, but the great commanders are determined to win through maneuver rather than attrition. As Sun Tzu put it, the greatest general is the one who can win without fighting.

In 327 BC, Alexander the Great set out to besiege an enemy stronghold known as the Sogdian Rock. A large army defended this fortress, which was surrounded by precipitous walls, and they were provisioned for a long siege. They believed their position to be impregnable.

When Alexander demanded their surrender, they replied that he had better find soldiers with wings, since that was all they had to fear. Alexander called for volunteers who were skilled at mountain-climbing and offered huge rewards to any who could make a summit

Your think ethic is as important as your work ethic

that overlooked the fortress before the sun rose the next day. Three hundred answered the call, and made a treacherous night climb, during which thirty men lost their lives. In the morning, they signaled down with flags to let Alexander know they had successfully reached the peak. Alexander then renewed his demand that the Sogdians surrender at once, stating that otherwise his "winged soldiers" would fly down upon them. When the Sogdians looked up and saw men in glistening armor standing on the "un-climbable" peak above, they immediately surrendered.

More than 2,000 years later, a young advertising executive named Gary Dahl met some friends in a bar. They were all talking about their pets, and when he arrived they asked if he had a pet. He replied that he had a pet rock, and that it required very little care and feeding. They all had a great laugh. Most people would have let it go at that. But Dahl went home and wrote a manual on the care and feeding of a pet rock. He designed a little cage in which people could keep their pet rocks, and a leash with which they could take their pet rocks out for a walk. Then he took his creation to the national convention of gift stores and started to sell them. One year later, Dahl was a multimillionaire and one of the classic American fads had been created.

America has always been a place where someone with a great work ethic could get ahead. A willingness to work hard will always be important, but in the world of today having a great "think ethic" is just as important, and often more important, than a great work ethic. And as the case of Gary Dahl and the Pet Rock shows, it can be a lot more lucrative and a lot more fun.

WINNING THE WAR WITH YOURSELF REQUIRES PHYSICAL STAMINA

When your body is strong it will bend to your commands. When your body is weak you must give into its demands.

Samurai aphorism

It's 6 o'clock in the morning, dark, and 26 degrees outside. You've just laced up your running shoes. You know what happens next, don't you? YOWE launches an all-out assault in a frantic effort to drive you back into the protective fortress of your warm bed.

If you're in shape you'll brush YOWE off the way a Sherman tank would brush off a wooden spear. Your body will do what you command it to do. And with that start on your day, you will be much more likely to be pleasant, positive, and productive all day long.

If you're not in shape, YOWE's assault will be the Sherman tank and your lack of determination will be the wooden spear. If you end up back under the covers, promising yourself that you'll run tomorrow (as if it's going to be any lighter or warmer the next morning), YOWE has won. And that early morning defeat might keep you on the defensive all day long.

Make your body obey when you tell it to move

It doesn't take much to stay one step ahead of YOWE. Give up one "reality" TV show and replace it with a real trip to the gym, a bike ride, or a fast walk. You'll feel better, look better, and get more done. And you'll send YOWE scurrying back to the foxhole.

TOUGH TIMES CALL FOR TOUGH LEADERS

The Lord of the Rings by J.R.R. Tolkien is one of the greatest stories ever written, and the movie adaptation by Peter Jackson is one of the great cinematic accomplishments of all time. As with all great fiction, there are many lessons woven throughout the story. In fact, although he did not intend it as such, I believe that Tolkien's classics are among the greatest leadership textbooks ever written if you are reading them for that purpose (I once wrote a book on leadership lessons from *The Hobbit* and *The Lord of the Rings*).

The greatest test of leadership is not the ability to build a team or grow a business, as important as these are. The greatest test is the ability to keep the team inspired and motivated when to all outside appearances the war has been lost. Almost to the very end of Tolkien's story, there is an oppressive sense that the forces of evil are so overwhelming that their victory is inevitable: when the Fellowship is confronted by the Balrog in the mines of Moria; during the sieges of Helm's Deep and Minas Tirith; when Sam and Frodo fall into the hands of orcs in Mordor. At these times, you want to close the book and weep for the fate of Middle-earth. And yet, at the darkest moments are being planted the seeds for ultimate victory. It is at these moments we most need resilient leadership.

One of the greatest tests of leadership in our recent history was the Great Depression. I believe that one of the most important sentences uttered during the 20th century was FDR's statement that we have nothing to fear but fear itself, because that speech brought an immediate end to bank runs that threatened the very fabric of our society. Six of the eight companies profiled in my book *All Hands on Deck: Eight Essential Lessons for Building a Culture of Ownership* lived through the Great Depression. Not one of them executed a layoff during those darkest of days; quite to the contrary, because of their resilient leadership they each emerged from that cauldron stronger, bigger, and poised for even greater achievements.

In today's turbulent environment, leaders are challenged to inspire their people with the courage and perseverance to deal with whatever the world throws at them. My vote for another of the most important sentences of the 20th century is Winston Churchill's "we shall never surrender!"

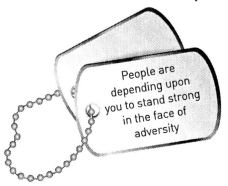

People are depending upon you to stand strong in the face of adversity

Historians have long debated the extent to which history is directed, or deflected, by the so-called "great man or woman." There are excellent arguments on both sides, but to the extent that the "great man or woman" theory does hold it is most pronounced during the toughest of times: George Washington at Valley Forge, Florence Nightingale at the Scutari Barrack Hospital, Anthony McAuliffe at the Battle of the Bulge. Tough times call for leaders who have the inner strength to stand tough, and to inspire followers to persevere through tough times.

BE HUMBLE

In his book *Why We Lost: A General's Inside Account of the Iraq and Afghanistan Wars*, Daniel Bolger wrote: "We faltered due to a distinct lack of humility. Certain we knew best, confident our skilled troops would prevail, we persisted in a failed course for far too long and came up well short, to the detriment of our trusting countrymen."

Jim Collins, author of such business books as *Built to Last* and *Good to Great*, describes five levels of leadership. At the pinnacle, Level 5 leadership is a paradoxical blend of incredibly strong determination to achieve goals coupled with genuine personal humility. Read about America's greatest military leaders – Washington, Grant, Eisenhower – and this quality shines through. It is no coincidence that each of these military leaders were sub-sequently trusted by their coun-trymen with two terms of office as President of the United States.

Arrogance is the pride that causes the fall

YOWE thrives on vanity and arrogance, on looking down your nose at other people, seeing yourself as one of the chosen few. And YOWE hates humility – saying you're sorry, saying you could be wrong, and occasionally following instead of always having to be the leader.

The culture of arrogance at Enron greatly contributed to the ethical and legal violations which caused that company's implosion. The personal arrogance of Lance Armstrong assured that when the truth finally came out about the way he'd lied about his use of performance-enhancing drugs he would, almost overnight, become one of the most despised men in America.

Arrogance is more than just the pride that comes before the fall — arrogance is often the root cause of the fall. And when you take that fall it will be YOWE standing behind you giving a push.

BE A SERVANT LEADER

One of my all-time favorite books is Steven Pressfield's *Gates of Fire: An Epic Novel of the Battle of Thermopylae.* There is a scene where Xeones, the story's narrator, describes what he knows about leadership from having watched Spartan King Leonidas lead his fellow Greeks in holding off a much larger Persian army for three days. He says:

> A king does not abide within his tent while his men bleed and die upon the field. A king does not dine while his men go hungry, nor sleep when they stand at watch upon the wall. A king does not command his men's loyalty through fear nor purchase it with gold; he earns their love by the sweat of his own back and the pains he endures for their sake. That which comprises the harshest burden, a king lifts first and sets down last. A king does not require service of those he leads but provides it to them. He serves them, not they him… A king does not expend his substance to enslave men, but by his conduct and example makes them free.

This is the most eloquent description of servant leadership I have ever read. It is also a great prescription for defeating YOWE. You see, when your attention is focused on serving others, self-interest and ego take a back seat. YOWE becomes marginalized. And your best self has a chance to shine through.

And the best part is that you don't have to be a king to follow this prescription. In fact, you don't need a title of any sort. Management is a job description. Your organization can make you a manager with a new job description and name tag, and perhaps a pay raise. Leadership is a life decision. A leader is someone who - through the expectations they establish and the example they set – influences and inspires others to follow.

SECURE YOUR VICTORY

Hadrian became Roman emperor upon the death of Trajan in 117 AD. Under Trajan the empire had reached its greatest geographic expanse, but there was rebellion percolating at multiple points and imperial finances were in shambles, largely as a result of the constant campaigning that had gone into acquiring and maintaining an ever-growing empire. Hadrian realized that Rome's ambitions had outstripped her resources, so he withdrew from some of the outlying provinces that were likely to require heavy military commitment to retain.

He then set about to secure the remaining empire. He fortified the borders, including Hadrian's Wall in England, traveled extensively to stay connected with his far-flung administrators and generals, reformed the civil service, and helped move the empire toward a commonwealth model. After his death in 138 AD, Rome enjoyed another four decades of peace, and on the foundation he helped to fortify, centuries more of dominance over Europe and the Mediterranean.

If you read every success strategy book that's been written by an athletic coach you will see many different philosophies with regard to recruiting, training, organization, and motivation, but every single coach who has ever led a team to the championship will agree on this one thing: it's easier to become a champion than it is to remain a champion, and after you've won it all is often the time of your greatest danger, because that's when arrogance and complacence are most likely to set in. Make certain to secure your victory.

EVERY TRUCE IS TEMPORARY

On Christmas Eve of 1914 an unsanctioned truce broke out on the Western Front. For five months the German troops on one side of No Man's Land and the British and French troops on the other side had been slaughtering each other under the most hideous conditions imaginable. But on that Christmas Eve German soldiers on the eastern side of no-man's land sang Silent Night loudly enough that the Brits could hear it. And on the western side of the blood-stained field of mud that separated the enemies, frontline Tommies joined in, each side harmonizing in its own language. The next morning a German soldier stood up on the rampart and waved to his enemies – and no British soldier shot at him.

Over the next several hours men emerged from the trenches and congregated in what had been, and soon again would return to being, the killing ground. They exchanged cigarettes and souvenirs, and in some places impromptu soccer games were staged. The fighting recommenced on the following day and over the next three and one-half years these men would kill each other by the millions. But for that one glorious morning there was peace.

Your war against YOWE will never end. The day you think you've conquered your inner enemy will be the day you become complacent and set yourself up for a fall. It's been said (by General George C. Marshall among others) that eternal vigilance is the price of peace. So it is in winning the war with yourself. You will win some battles, you will lose some battles. You will occasionally agree to a truce with YOWE. On occasion YOWE might even become your temporary ally by goading or shaming you into taking some needed action like losing weight or changing your spending habits.

But don't trust YOWE to stay on your side.

In 1939 Joseph Stalin had convinced himself that Adolph Hitler was his ally. Even as the German Wehrmacht was massing on Soviet borders, Russian trains were transporting raw materials across those borders into Germany. Millions of Russians, Ukrainians, and other nationalities then under the thumb of the Soviet empire paid with their lives for their leader's complacence and self-delusion.

The day after the Christmas truce of 1914 the fighting resumed. Remember that. Every truce you have with YOWE will be temporary. As soon as you let down your guard, YOWE will launch a sneak attack.

PROSILIENCE AND THE PARADOX OF MOTIVATION

General Douglas MacArthur said that two words could be used to describe the cause of virtually every calamitous defeat in warfare: Too late.

Those two words can also sum up the paradox of motivation. It's easy to be motivated when things are going great. It's also largely irrelevant because things are already going great. When you've just gotten a promotion and a pay raise, there's money in the bank, the kids are doing well in school and you're looking forward to a well-earned vacation, you don't need an inspirational book or motivational audio to get you fired up because you already are.

It's hardest to be motivated when things are falling apart. It's when you've lost the job, you don't know how you're going to make your mortgage payments, you've just learned that your kid's been arrested for punching his probation officer, and the closest you're going to come to a vacation is an hour with your therapist, that you most need the inspirational book and the motivational audio. Unfortunately, that's also the time when the message is least likely to have an impact. It was too late.

Ironically, it's also when you've hit bottom that a shot of motivation can have the greatest leverage. That's when the person who's just lost a job summons up the courage to finally start the business she's always dreamed about starting. It's when the alcoholic finally summons the courage to stand in front of a roomful of other drunks and admit to needing their help. It's when the profligate spender finally buys Dave Ramsey's book and embarks upon a total money makeover.

John F. Kennedy said the time to patch the roof is when the sun is shining. The time to work on being resilient, motivated, and self-empowered is when you're already feeling resilient, motivated, and self-empowered.

You need to practice Prosilience. Now, don't go running to your dictionary to look that work up. It's not there – at least not yet. I made it up. Prosilience is Prospective Resilience. Resilience that is developed in advance of its being called upon. It's preparing for the inevitable

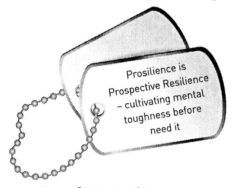

Prosilience is
Prospective Resilience
– cultivating mental
toughness before
need it

obstacles, setbacks, and adversities of life *before* the occur (and occur they will) because if you wait until you need to be resilient to work on the skills required for resilience, you might well find that you waited too long.

In Part 3, I'll share the seven promises of The Self-Empowerment Pledge. I'm going to encourage you to repeat each day's promise at least four times on that day, and to keep doing it until you have learned them by heart, until they have become part of your mental and emotional DNA.

Every time you repeat one of the promises to yourself, you'll hear YOWE scoffing – or howling – that you don't need these promises, that you already get it. But by now you know exactly what YOWE is up to. So ignore that voice and keep promising yourself to be responsible, accountable, determined, generous, resilient, positive, and faithful.

Because if you wait till you need it, you just might find that it's too late.

DON'T MARCH IN THE MARCH OF FOLLY

"Folly often does not spring from a great design and its consequences are frequently a surprise. The folly lies in persisting {after the consequences of folly have become apparent}."

Barbara Tuchman: *The March of Folly: From Troy to Vietnam*

In *The March of Folly* Barbara Tuchman describes historical examples of political and military leaders acting in ways that were – and should have been recognized as being – antithetical to the highest interests of their nations (and for that matter of themselves personally).

In describing the tragedy of U.S. involvement in the Vietnam War (which in Vietnam is remembered as the American War, which followed hard on the heels of the French War), Tuchman recounts four persistent follies that resulted in a war that caused 45,000 American deaths and 300,000 wounded and over $150 billion beyond what a normal military budget would have been - all "sacrificed for nothing."

The first folly was persistent overreacting – for example creating a perception that the security of the United States was threatened by what was happening in jungles 8,000 miles away, that the fall of South Vietnam to communist forces would somehow result in a "domino effect" that would automatically sweep the rest of the region into the sway of the hammer and sickle.

The second folly was "the illusion of omnipotence." In particular this was reflected in the fatally-flawed belief that the American superpower could simultaneously win the hearts and minds of the Vietnamese people in "nation building" while devastating their countryside with napalm, carpet bombing and search-and-destroy missions.

The third folly was what Tuchman calls "wooden-headedness" – refusing to objectively perceive the facts. In particular, she says, this was reflected in the way American policy-makers ignored the eminently demonstrated commitment of the North Vietnamese to persist in the fight no matter what level of pain was inflicted upon their society by American firepower.

And the fourth folly she described was "the absence of reflective thought about what we were doing, about effectiveness in relation to the object sought, about balance of possible gain as against loss and against harm to both [South Vietnam] and to the United States."

Overreacting to the situation. Delusions of grandeur. Seeing what you want to see. Not thinking things before acting. It all sounds like the work of YOWE, doesn't it?

In Part 3 we'll see how making the seven promises of The Self Empowerment Pledge can help you defeat YOWE and prevent it from leading you down the march of folly.

PART 3

THE SELF
EMPOWERMENT
PLEDGE

"No empowerment is so effective as self-empowerment... In this world, the optimists have it, not because they are always right, but because they are always positive. Even when wrong, they are positive, and that is the way of achievement, correction, improvement, and success. Educated, eyes-open optimism pays; pessimism can only offer the empty consolation of being right {because it creates a self-fulfilling prophecy of failure}."

David Landes: "Culture Makes All the Difference" in *Culture Matters: How Values Shape Human Progress* (edited by Samuel P. Huntington and Lawrence E. Harrison)

THE SELF EMPOWERMENT PLEDGE

"I attribute my success to the fact that I never gave or took an excuse."

- Florence Nightingale

Nobody else will, or could even if they wanted to, "empower" you to conquer YOWE – to win the war with yourself. It is and always will be an inside job. If someone can give you empowerment they can also take it away, and loaned empowerment is not the real thing. But when you have empowered yourself, no one can take that power away from you.

Self empowerment is a commitment that you make to not be deterred from achieving your most important goals and from becoming your authentic best self.

The seven Promises – one for each day of the week – of The Self-Empowerment Pledge are a powerful weapon for subduing YOWE. Each Promise represents the antithesis of what YOWE wants you to do:

» *Monday's Promise is Responsibility:* YOWE refuses to accept personal responsibility for anything and is always ready with an excuse to make or a finger to point to rationalize away the fact that you have given up on the dream you once had and have settled for being a lesser version of your best self.

» *Tuesday's Promise is Accountability:* YOWE deploys low self-esteem, self-limiting beliefs, and pathological concern for the opinions of other people to keep you from dreaming big dreams, taking courageous stands, committing yourself to a transcendent purpose, and doing the work required to be your best self.

» *Wednesday's Promise is Determination:* YOWE is a coward and a quitter and will use every weapon in its arsenal to keep you frightened and paralyzed, and to prevent you from doing the things you are afraid to do and from asking for help when you need it.

» *Thursday's Promise is Contribution:* YOWE's dial is perpetually tuned to radio station WIIFM – What's In It For Me? – and seeks to transform your every charitable inclination into a return on investment calculation.

» *Friday's Promise is Resilience:* YOWE takes rejection and failure as a reflection of personal inadequacy or as a symptom of a hostile world and uses these experiences as a cattle prod to force you back onto the couch with a TV remote in your hand.

» *Saturday's Promise is Perspective:* For YOWE the glass is always half empty – and leaking from a hole in the bottom. It exploits every adversity as another opportunity to weaken you and turn you into a victim rather than to see you grow stronger and wiser from the experience.

» *Sunday's Promise is Faith:* Gratitude is an absolutely foreign concept to YOWE, who would much rather keep you in a state of resentment for what you don't have rather than appreciating all that you have been blessed with.

TAKE THE PLEDGE – MAKE THE PROMISES

If you knew that it would change your life in a profound, positive, and permanent way, over the next year would you invest 365 minutes in yourself? Would you invest one minute a day for a year if you knew it would help you achieve your goals and help you become a better person?

If your answer is yes, here's what you do. Make copies of The Self-Empowerment Pledge (it can be downloaded for free at www. PledgePower.com) and place them where you'll see them often: the bathroom mirror, on the wall where you work, your locker at the gym, the seat of your car. First thing every morning repeat that day's Promise to yourself. That will take you about 15 seconds. Do it again mid-day, one more time at the end of your work day, and one more time right before you go to bed. Do it out loud whenever possible.

Four times 15 seconds – one minute a day. Repeat the Promise with conviction, like you really mean it. Put on your war face and do it looking in the mirror.

For the first several months you'll hear a little voice in the back of your head laugh deviously and say "like hell you will." But now you know that's the voice of YOWE trying to prevent you from growing, so tell it to shut up and keep on making the Promises. At some point you won't have to read them anymore because you'll know them by heart. Not from memory – *by heart*.

Here's what will happen: the more deeply those Promises become embedded in your mind (as a result of repetition), the more obvious and painful it will be when you catch yourself breaking them – something that at least initially will happen many times a day.

You will start to develop what psychologists call cognitive dissonance – trying to hold two incompatible beliefs at the same time. "I am responsible, accountable, determined and resilient" cannot exist in the same mental space with "It's not my fault, I give up, and I'll get around to it tomorrow."

Cognitive dissonance is a form of mental illness, except in this case it's being used in a healthy and constructive manner – if and only if it inspires you to make the changes necessary to start doing a better job of living the Promises. As the cognitive dissonance becomes more intense, one of three things *must* happen. First, you could decide that mental illness is not so bad after all – that you'll keep making the promises, keep breaking them, and just live with cognitive dissonance and you're okay with that. Second, you take the easy way out and just stop making the promises. But if you keep making the promises in good faith, then you must begin to change your attitudes and behaviors. As you do that, you'll start seeing more positive results and the process will become self-reinforcing.

YOWE will howl and swear. YOWE will accuse you of having joined a sinister cult and of "drinking the Kool-Aid." YOWE will whimper that at one minute a day for a year you will have missed 365 TV commercials!

Every time you ignore YOWE and make one of the Promises, every time you keep one of these promises even though YOWE does everything in its power to stop you, you become stronger and YOWE grows weaker.

We have seen people make amazing – even miraculous – changes in their lives as a result of making a daily commitment to the seven promises of The Self Empowerment Pledge. We've seen people get out of debt, lose weight, change relationships, and finally undertake long postponed dreams such as writing their book, starting their business, or applying to graduate school.

When Values Coach introduced The Self Empowerment Pledge at Midland Health in West Texas, managers around the hospital began to include daily recitation of that day's promise into staff meetings, nursing unit huddles, and impromptu gatherings. As is always the case, there was initial resistance on the part of some employees who thought it was silly. Of course, the resistance is often the most tenacious from precisely the people who could most benefit from taking these seven promises to heart.

In a story recounted in *Chicken Soup for the Soul: Inspiration for Nurses: 101 Stories of Appreciation and Wisdom* by Amy Newmark and LeAnn Thieman, Midland Health's Chief Operating Officer Bob Dent tells the story of Kyle, a nurse who had been stealing narcotics from his unit's medication room for his own personal use because he was a drug addict. Eventually, verbally making those promises every morning and then watching himself break them every afternoon became such a painful thing that he couldn't live with himself. He and his wife came in to see Bob and in an emotional meeting he confessed to what he'd been doing. The hospital sent him through a 30-day drug treatment program and as of this writing Kyle is approaching his second year of being drug-free and serving as a positive example for many others. The word he used to describe the changes he'd empowered himself to make is miracle.

RECRUIT A PLEDGEPARTNER

Recruiting a PledgePartner will help you leverage your efforts and accelerate your progress. It should be someone you trust and respect, but who is also willing to help you hold yourself to your commitments. Each of you should sign a contract – you can use the template I've included here.

PledgePartner Agreement

This agreement signifies the fact that we are both committed to being better people and to making our corner of the world a better place by taking and keeping the seven promises of The Self Empowerment Pledge. In that spirit we will support and encourage each other by doing these things:

» Share with each other one personal, professional, spiritual, or other goal that The Self Empowerment Pledge will help us to achieve.

» Commit to each other that over a pre-determined period of 21 days we will each watch that day's lesson from the PledgePower course.

» During those 21 days we will each send the other a brief message of encouragement, periodically including an update on progress toward keeping the promises and achieving the goal, by telephone, email, text, or in person. Good intentions and telepathy do not count.

» Once a week during those 21 days we will schedule a phone call, skype session, or face-to-face meeting for an open and honest conversation about successes, frustrations, and what more we can do for each other to help stay on track with our promises.

» After the end of the 21-day course we will each message each other via email, text, phone call or other method, and at least once a month we will schedule a phone call or face-to-face meeting.

» We will honor the commitments to listen without judging and to hold everything that we share with one another in the strictest confidence.

Signature	Date	Signature	Date

PLEDGEPOWER

PledgePower.com

Every day, seven days a week, I send my PledgePartner a text letting him know whether or not I kept the commitment I've made to devote two uninterrupted hours a day to writing. The first time I had to tell him I'd failed to meet the commitment I didn't even need to wait for his response to know that on the following day my text would read:

That commitment to two hours per day – a commitment that I've made to my PledgePartner and to my self – is the reason you are reading this book.

Monday's Promise is Responsibility

Self-empowerment begins with personal responsibility, and that's a two-way street: you are both responsible to and responsible for. You are responsible *to* your boss, your co-workers, your spouse, the IRS, and so forth. You are responsible *for* providing for your family, managing your finances, doing good work, taking care of your health, and so forth. We begin with Responsibility because accepting complete responsibility for your health, happiness, success, and life is the essential and non-negotiable step toward being a mature and self-empowered adult.

To be responsible means that you are able to respond. You compromise your ability to respond when you procrastinate, make excuses, blame other people for your problems and predicaments, or in any other way play the victim or the martyr.

Responsibility means making a commitment to eliminate the ex's in your life: no excuses, no exceptions, no exemptions, no extensions, no extenuations. And no blaming the ex: the ex-spouse, ex-boss, ex-anyone else.

Responsibility means embracing the fact that you are where you are today because of choices you have made in the past *and no other reason*. It means embracing the fact that your future will be determined by choices you make from this day forward *and no other reason*. It means that you accept complete and total responsibility for your present circumstances and your future outcomes.

As long as you are waiting for someone else to solve your problems for you, making excuses for not having effectively dealt with those problems, and blaming other people (or God or fate) for the fact that you have problems, you are sinking into the victim role – practicing what psychologists call learned helplessness. When you accept complete and total responsibility for your health, your happiness, your success, and your life you stop blaming "the diet" for the fact that you didn't lose any weight and you stop waiting for Uncle Lotto to fix all your problems with a winning lottery ticket. Instead you buckle down and do the work that must be done to improve your health and your financial prosperity.

One more thing – the difference between a problem and a predicament: A problem has a solution, a predicament does not. A problem is an alcoholic neighbor disturbing the peace – a predicament is an alcoholic mother-in-law living upstairs. You can deal with a problem, but you must learn to live with a predicament. To be responsible means you don't bitch, moan, whine or complain (that *other* BMW Club) about either one. Live with it or deal with it – don't play victim or martyr because of it.

TUESDAY'S PROMISE IS ACCOUNTABILITY

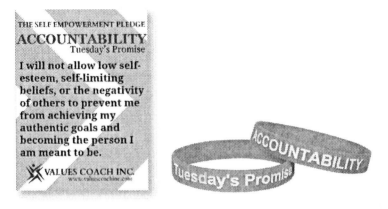

Full disclosure: Of all seven promises of The Self Empowerment Pledge, this one is for me the most challenging to keep. In all likelihood that will also be the case for you. But I will also tell you this – the degree to which I am able to keep this promise made to myself, the more effectively I am able to keep the other six promises. In all likelihood that will also be the case for you.

Low self-esteem, self-limiting beliefs, and pathological worrying about what you think other people might think of you are three of YOWE's most potent weapons preventing you from taking risks, asking for help, and taking action to achieve your goals, realize your dreams, and fulfill your destiny.

Not liking yourself, not believing in yourself, and assuming that other people don't like you or believe in you can become a deterrent more powerful than any brick wall or iron bars you will ever run into. These qualities end up being your excuse for laziness and cowardice. You don't try because you assume that you'll fail; you don't ask because you assume you'll be rejected.

To keep this promise you must be tough *with* yourself by holding yourself to high standards and expectations, but not be tough *on* yourself when you don't always live up to those standards and expectations.

When you hold yourself accountable, you don't have to worry about other people doing it for you by looking over your shoulder, cracking the whip at your back, or holding your feet to the fire.

Keep this promise for long enough and it will change everything: How you see yourself, how you face challenges and pursue opportunities, and the confidence level you have in building relationships with others.

WEDNESDAY'S PROMISE IS DETERMINATION

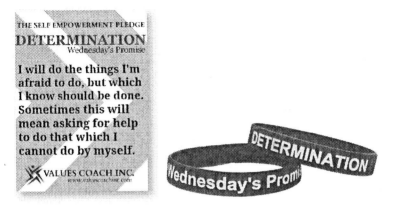

Several years ago I received a call from a man who worked at a large financial services company. He reminded me that we'd met when I'd conducted a workshop for his company earlier in the year. I remembered him because he was very proud of being the #1 producer in the entire company. He told me that if the world was fair he would be sending me a check for $10,000.

That got my attention. Tell me why, I said.

"Wednesday's Promise," he replied. He went on to say that for him that wasn't just Wednesday's Promise, it was his seven days a week promise. He had it taped to his bathroom mirror, on his locker at the gym, under the glass of his desk at work; he'd even laminated a copy and left it on the seat of his car as a reminder every time he got in to drive somewhere.

"It's been amazing," he said. "I'm making calls that I used to be afraid to make. When I talk to people I'm asking them to buy the product instead of telling them to think about it. I'm asking other people to help me open doors at prospects that I used to think were too big to go after. My sales rate – and my income – have increased substantially, and if the world was fair you'd be getting a commission."

Then he reminded me that during my presentation I'd said that the world is *not* always fair, and that I would not be receiving a commission check (which I would not have accepted in any event).

What's your most important goal? Doubling your income? Losing weight? Writing the Great American Novel? Seeing the Great Wall of China?

Whatever the goal, internalizing Wednesday's Promise on Determination will help you achieve it. On the other hand, if you are unwilling to do the things you're afraid to do and to ask for help when you need it, those big goals are likely to deteriorate into fantasy daydreams.

YOWE loves fantasy daydreams.

Thursday's Promise is Contribution

I am periodically in a position to advise someone who has lost a job. (I always stress that they lost *a* job – it was not really *their* job). I tell them they should treat finding another job as a full-time job – but with this structure: four days a week they should work on their own job search but one day a week they should devote themselves to helping someone else who is out of work. Someday, I assure them, they will look back on the one day spent helping others as having been more important to their own career success than the four days they spent on their own job search.

A while back I was helping someone whose executive position at a large hospitality company had been eliminated. In addition to sharing the 4-to-1 job search formula, I asked him to describe his dream job: what sort of company he would be working for, what he would be doing, where he would live, even the sort of car he would be driving.

Several years later I got a call from the man. He had just moved to Florida to begin work in the dream job he'd described during our meeting, working for the company that had been at the top of his list. And he'd just bought a sporty new convertible.

But this isn't a story about visualizing abundance – it's a story about making a contribution. The man who'd hired him into this dream job was someone who, several years before, my friend had helped get back on his feet after he'd been fired. "It's true," my friend told me. "What goes around does come around – eventually." I have a framed saying in my office. I call it Rafe's Law because it's something that Rafe, a character in my book *Never Fear, Never Quit,* said was a universal principle of the cosmos. It says:

Whatever you most need in life, the best way for you to get it is to help someone else get it who needs it more than you do.

If you've just lost a job, reach out to help someone else who's been unemployed for a year. If you're worried about paying the mortgage, volunteer at the local homeless shelter. If you can't get yourself started on writing the Great American Novel, encourage someone else who's stuck in writer's block. What goes around really does come around.

FRIDAY'S PROMISE IS RESILIENCE

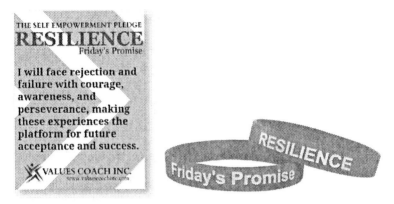

In life, rejection is The Red Badge of Courage. Cowards don't get rejected very often because they don't have the courage to ask. The people who consistently bounce back from rejection are the ones who are trying to achieve big goals, who are trying to change the world.

And in life, failure is the Medal of Honor. Cowards don't fail very often because they don't have the courage to try. The heroes of our world are the ones who trip and fall, get up and dust themselves off, and – wiser and stronger for the experience – charge once more into the breach.

It's human nature to take rejection personally, but when the answer is no, it's almost never *you* that's been rejected. When an employer decides to hire someone with a more relevant resume, they are not rejecting *you*. When a publisher concludes that they wouldn't be able to sell a sufficient number of your books to cover the cost, they are not rejecting *you*. When a prospect decides that the product or service you are selling doesn't meet their needs, they are not rejecting *you*.

When the answer is no, do what you can to understand why the other person isn't buying what you are selling, but remember that it was not *you* being rejected. When you personalize rejection, you are making YOWE King or Queen for a day. Unfortunately, because

YOWE loves being on that throne, it will cause you to act in ways that bring about even more rejection in the future. By now I hope you're seeing this pattern clearly – YOWE wins by making you lose.

In his book *Whoever Makes the Most Mistakes Wins*, Richard Farson wrote that it's not really failure that we fear – what we really fear is the humiliation of being seen as a failure. But again, that's just YOWE trying to perch tall on that throne at the center of the universe. Remember – you will worry a lot less about what other people think of you if you will acknowledge how *infrequently* other people think of you.

SATURDAY'S PROMISE IS PERSPECTIVE

Is it the best of times or the worst of times? The answer to that question is always yes. It depends upon what you choose to see, and the light in which you choose to see it. The operative word here is choose.

Do you choose to see the best of times or the worst of times?

Do you choose to see the best in other people or to look for their faults and flaws?

When the answer is no, do you take it personally or do you hit the "next" button and move on?

At one point I caught myself thinking that every time I came up for air it felt like a giant thumb came down and pushed me back under. Then it struck me that I could as easily have said that every time I got pushed under it felt like a giant palm lifted me back up to take a breath. Same circumstances but a different metaphor created a completely different perspective.

The perspective you choose to have will determine whether you see your work as a privilege or a burden. And make no mistake that this is a choice you make and not a matter of status and paycheck. I know senior executives who dread going to work and housekeepers who embody Kahlil Gibran's aphorism that work is love made visible. Which one are you?

SUNDAY'S PROMISE IS FAITH

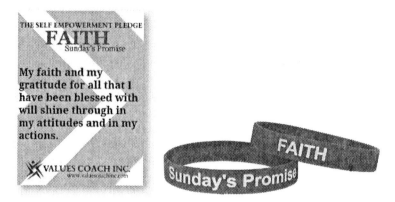

In the context of The Self-Empowerment Pledge is not about religious belief or dogma. This is the faith that we all need, regardless of our specific belief or non-belief. The four pillars of faith are faith in yourself, faith in other people, faith in the future, and faith in something higher than the almighty dollar and trying to win by dying with the most toys.

Faith in yourself is your most powerful weapon for fighting the low self-esteem and poor self-image that YOWE uses to keep that basket of mediocrity firmly planted over the candle of your innate brilliance.

Faith in other people is your most powerful weapon for combatting the cynicism, suspicion, and arrogance that YOWE uses to keep you feeling isolated and alone in a hostile world.

Faith in the future is your most powerful weapon for overcoming the anxiety and pessimism that YOWE uses to keep you firmly planted in the status quo of your comfort zone and to prevent you from dreaming big and taking risks.

Faith in something more than the material world – what some call a higher power and some call God – is your most powerful weapon to resist YOWE's insistence that you are the center of the universe – that it really is all about you.

In the conclusion to her book *A History of God* Karen Armstrong wrote: "The very nature of humanity...demands that we transcend ourselves and our current perceptions, and this principle indicates the presence of what has been called the divine in the very nature of serious human inquiry." Because we humans cannot long endure emptiness and desolation, she writes, we will – we must – fill the vacuum "by creating a new focus of meaning."

This brings us back to the eternal struggle between ego and soul that I described at the beginning of the book. Whether or not you win the war with yourself will ultimately be determined by which part of "you" you allow to fill that vacuum: YOWE or your authentic best self.

My favorite Bible verse is Mark 9:23 – All things are possible for one who believes. If you read the passage carefully, it's clear that Jesus was not talking about believing the things that have been central to Christian religious teaching. At the time of this story, when Jesus was speaking to that desperate father of an epileptic son, not even his disciples had any inkling of virgin birth, resurrection or the other miracles that were subsequently to be woven into Christian religious dogma. I think Jesus was talking about faith in a larger general sense, not belief in a smaller particular sense. "I believe," said the father. "Help me overcome my unbelief."

Faith takes its first steps at the point where certainty ends.

YOWE wants the sure thing, the safe bet, the guarantee. That's why it fights so hard to keep you trapped in that prison cell with no lock on the door, euphemistically called the comfort zone.

It takes faith to keep walking when there's no guarantee that the path you're on doesn't lead to a dead end. It takes faith to make a decision, make a commitment, take a risk, take action when you're enshrouded in the fog of war. It takes faith to take the basket off your candle and become the person you are meant to be. It takes faith to conquer YOWE.

PART 4

THIS WAR
IS NEVER OVER

*The war with YOWE will never end
so don't let complacence stop you short of the finish line or let
fear stop you from getting up each time you fall down.*

THE WAR IS NEVER OVER...

So don't stop short of the finish line

Alexander the Great decisively defeated a much larger Persian army in the battle of the Granicus River, but that was at least partially a self-inflicted loss on the part of the Persians. A Persian attack force had made its way to the rear of Alexander's army and was poised to inflict serious damage. But instead of continuing their attack, the Persians stopped to plunder the Macedonians' baggage train. By stopping short of the finish line, they lost the battle – and most of them lost their lives. "Run through the tape," say track and field coaches, and it's good advice for all of us in our work and in our lives. Thomas Edison said that people would be appalled if they knew how close to the finish line they were when they quit – they did not run through the tape.

In the novel *1984*, George Orwell described a world of war without end. That happens to describe your relationship with Your Own Worst Enemy. There will be moments of truce, perhaps even extended periods of peaceful coexistence, but as soon as you think the war is over, that you have achieved ultimate victory, YOWE will emerge like a guerrilla fighter from the hills to knock you down a peg or two.

Never allow despair to stop you from fighting before the war has really been lost.

Never allow complacence to stop you from fighting before the war has really been won.

And this war is never over.

TAKE THE BASKET OFF YOUR CANDLE

You are living the one and only life you will be blessed with on this earth. Never look in the mirror and pretend to see less than what's really there looking back at you. Never settle for anemic dreams and goals because YOWE has convinced you that you're not capable of more, that you don't deserve more.

Take the basket off your inner candle and let it shine brightly. Become your meant to be best self. Pursue your most authentic dreams and goals with passion. Stop waiting for someone else to "empower" you and claim the God-given power that you were born with. Take action, take a risk, make a contribution, make a difference.

You owe it to yourself. You owe it to your family and to those you serve. You owe it to the world.

For the advanced course on
The Self Empowerment Pledge
sign up for PledgePower.

1 Pledge,
7 Promises,
21 Days

that will
change your life.

PLEDGE**POWER**

PledgePower.com